DUMFRIES AND GALLOWAY
HIGHWAYS AND BYWAYS

GUIDE TO
200
WALKS & CLIMBS

by R.D. WALTON

based on an earlier edition
by HENRY TRUCKELL

SEVENTH EDITION -- REVISED 1989

with route maps, section map

Photographs by R.D. WALTON

FOR RAMBLERS, TOURISTS, CYCLISTS
and PONY TREKKERS

T.C. FARRIES and CO. LIMITED
1989

First published in U.K. 1935

7th Revised Edition 1989 — T.C. Farries & Co. Ltd.

ISBN 0 948278 12.9

Printed and bound by R. Booth, Bookbinder Ltd, Mabe, Penryn,
Cornwall

Front Cover : Loch Arthur and Beeswing

Foreword
by Sir Hector Monro, D.L., M.P.

Anyone who is able to take a few of Mr Walton's walks in Dumfries and Galloway will most certainly be opening the door to some of the most beautiful and unspoilt countryside in Scotland.

The Queensway and the Southern Upland Way initiated by the Forestry Commission and the Countryside Commission are well-known routes. Mr Walton offers the alternatives. He frequently takes us off the beaten track to picturesque areas many perhaps did not know existed.

However he has kept many of his walks to a comfortable distance that can be covered in a day or less. Many hill walkers and mountaineers set out over the years to climb all 'the Munros' in Scotland. It would seem to me that it will be a splendid objective to cover all the 200 'Waltons' in Dumfries and Galloway. I am sure every walk will be well worthwhile, and remembered and relived for many years to come.

I believe Mr R.D. Walton's walks will give great happiness to an ever growing army of enthusiasts who like rambling in the countryside. His warning to treat it carefully is important. It is precious and it is our heritage.

Good walking to you all.

Most of the new walks in this revised edition are designed for those who wish shorter walks rather than strenuous hiking and each aims at some interesting or historical feature. Such are the walks to Orchardton Tower, Threave Castle, Carron Linn, Morton Castle, Drumlanrig Castle grounds, the four Memorial Monuments, the Deil's Dyke, Barrs Hill Fort, the Glenkiln statues, Dalry new footbridge, Dalswinton Loch.

PREFACE

The increased traffic on most of the roads in Dumfries and Galloway has made walks on these roads less than attractive. Walks have therefore been arranged in groups from starting points that can be reached by car or sometimes by bus, and routes on busy roads are mostly avoided. Most of the routes given are circular, but some are best done as 'through' routes if a driver can be arranged to take a car to the other end, or as 'cross-over' routes by arranging with another party to do the walk in the opposite direction and exchange cars for the return journey.

Some walks are very short, suitable for a winter afternoon or a summer evening. Paths that are easy to follow in winter or spring become overgrown in summer and autumn and may be difficult to follow.

Forestry roads and tracks increase yearly and are usually available for walkers. Some of these have been detailed, but usually a number of entrance points have been given and walks of various lengths can be made from these. The Forestry Commission has published a number of booklets giving details of a few short walks in some of the forests.

Map references are given in the standard six figure reference system and the Ordnance Survey 1 : 50,000 maps are recommended. For greater detail in an area of special interest, the small sheets of the 1 : 25,000 Ordnance maps are invaluable; and for a more general view of a larger area the ½ inch maps of Bartholomew's are useful. Heights are still given in feet.

Earlier editions of the Ordnance Survey maps, 50,000, 25,000, 1 inch or 2½ inch over the last many years showed footpaths by dotted lines. Many of these have vanished from the new 1987 sheets, to the great loss of walkers. Also striking features like the Deil's Dyke at Sanquhar and elsewhere have been removed from the maps. Hence the older maps may in some ways be found more useful.

The walking conditions likely to be met with are summarised as follows:

R	Road fit for cars, not necessarily public.
T	Rough track fit for landrovers or tractors.
P	Path for at least part of the way.
N	No path for some of the route, although usually R T or P at the ends.
C	Circular — starts and finishes at the same place.
(X)	a through walk or cross-over.
	In many cases C and (X) may be interchanged by altering travelling arrangements.
*	a hill climb.

Distances given are approximate, and on rough ground often feel more than as measured on the map. All the walks of types T N P are liable to be rough and muddy; for these, boots are recommended as both safer and more comfortable.

Some of the routes mentioned in this booklet are rights of way but there may be some which are not, and the inclusion of a route does not imply that it is a right of way. But, on the other hand, if care is taken not to damage crops or fences, to close gates and not to disturb livestock by taking a dog; if care is taken not to disturb sheep and lambs at or near lambing time, the majority of farmers and landowners are likely to regard you as inoffensive walkers. If, however, you use a car as a means of transport to the start of your walk it is important to make sure that you do not leave it where it obstructs the entrance or exit of a house, farm or field; if in doubt about where to leave a car it is better to ask if there is any objection.

It should also be noted that in order to reduce the damage done to dry-stane dykes by animals, human and other, there has been a great increase in the number of both barbed wire and electric fences. Determined walkers now carry a piece of rubberised fabric with them to overcome these difficulties, but a dry jerkin or empty rucksack can be just as effective. But also note that often a gate or a stile will be found nearby.

On the subject of litter, please carry back home all wrappings, cans, bottles and picnic debris you have brought with you and perhaps even something that others less thoughtful have left behind them. Adopt the advice of the Sierra Club of the USA:-

'Take only photographs
Leave only footprints."

5

R.D. WALTON

CONTENTS

SECTION 1   Near Dumfries

SECTION 2   The region between the New Abbey Road A710, the Dalbeattie Road A711 and the coast

SECTION 3   Region between the Dalbeattie Road A711 and the Castle-Douglas Road A75

SECTION 9   The region bounded by the Nith Valley on the west, the road to Wanlockhead and Leadhills B797, and the Moffat Road A701

4 Glencaple, Bankend, Kirkconnell Lea, Glencaple.. RC
5 Across the Lochar Moss .... TP(X) or C
6 Brow Well, Ruthwell, Bowerhouses, Clarencefield.. RTRC
7 Lochmaben, Hartwood, Torthorwald, Lochmaben .... RTRC
8 Breconrae, Holmains, Carthat, Breconrae ..... RTNTRC
9 Lanarkland, Bowhouse, Caerlaverock .... RTRC
10 Birrenswark or Burnswark Roman Camp ..... TRNTRC
11 Hazelshaw Hill and Blountfield .... TNPTRC
12 Raehills, Minnygap, Mollin, St. Ann's......... RPRC
13 Barrs Hill Fort .... RPN

SECTION 12   Wigtownshire
1 Stairhaven to Auchenmalg.................... NRC
2 St Ninian's Cave.............................. RTC
3 Burrow Head.................................. TNTC
4 Crammag Head .... RTNC
5 Clanyard Bay.................................. TNTC
6 Port Gill and Port Logan .... NTC
7 Black Head and Killantringan .... TNTRC
8 Loch Ochiltree .... RPC
9 Port Gill to Port Logan .... RNC
10 New England Bay to Balgown .... NRC
11 Carleton Shore .... RTNC
12 Garlieston - Eggerness Point .... TPNC

NOTE ON THE SOUTHERN UPLAND WAY
Walkers on The Southern Upland Way will find that there are
several places on The Way from which walks described in this
booklet may readily be tackled. Some may be done as side
excursions on a 'rest day' or as loop diversions. They are as follows:-

Section	Numbers
5	9, 10, 12, 13
6	1, 2, 11
7	1, 2, 3, 4, 5, 6, 7, 8, 9, 10, 11, 12, 15, 16
8	8, 11, 12, 13, 14, 15
10	1, 2, 3, 4, 5, 6, 7, 8, 9, 10, 12
12	7, 8

14

How lovely, Nith, thy fruitful vales,
Where bounding hawthorns gayly bloom;
And sweetly spread thy sloping dales,
Where lambkins wanton through the broom.
May there my latest hours consume!

BURNS

SECTION 1
Near Dumfries

See p.125 for note on places with Burns connections.

For most of the walks in this section the starting point is best reached by car or bus. It is possible to walk out from Dumfries, but this will be on a busy traffic route and will also add considerably to the distance. Also, where the route is circular (C) it is possible to start at any convenient point on it, and to go round in either direction.

1 Up the Nith. Greensands, Burns' Walk, Dalscone   PT

This is an attractive short walk from the centre of the town. A start may be made at the Buccleuch Street Bridge by going on to the path up the river just beside the Tourist Information Office. Access to or from this path is possible also at the Swimming Baths, from opposite Lovers' Walk, at the Albany road junction and at Nunholm, but the most attractive section is the part from Nunholm to Dalscone. The middle section of the walk is the part know as 'Burns' Walk'. It is necessary to leave the river bank at Albany and go along to the river. At Dalscone a track goes up to the right, past the farm and on to the Moffat Road (A701) just opposite a convenient bus stop back to town. Distance, about 2½-3 miles.

2 Up the Nith. Dalscone, Carnsalloch, Heathhall   TPRC

Leave the Moffat Road (A701) at Dalscone as in No. 1. A track leads past the farm down to the river bank and on to the raised embankment on the east side. This embankment may be followed pleasantly and easily for about 1½ miles to where a tributary burn comes in on the right. The path here turns right and goes past Carnsalloch Home to the road from Kirkton. Here turn right along the road for Heathhall and then right again down the Moffat Road back to the starting point. Distance, about 4½ miles.

15

3 St Queran's Well   PRC

Go down the New Abbey Road (A710) to Islesteps. On the west side of the bridge a stile between two houses leads to a path up the hillside and over a small crest to the Carruchan road. Cross this by two more stiles and continue by the edge of a wood downhill to the Crooks Pow. The well lies a few yards from the edge of the burn. It is reputed to be an ancient wishing well, dedicated to an Irish saint, Querdon. The path continues to join the Moss Road at (954 719). Turn left here, then left again at the New Abbey Road and return by it in about 1½ miles to the start at Islesteps. Distance, about 3 miles.

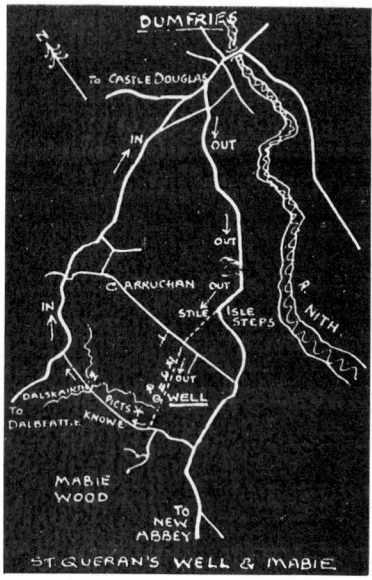

4   Carruchan Beeches and Moss Road   RC

This walk is all on tarred roads but only short stretches are busy. A start may be made at any suitable point on the circuit. If a start is made from the south end of the Moss Road at the junction with New Abbey Road (959 711) the latter is followed for half a mile north to the Flatts of Cargen roadend. Turn left uphill along the straight. almost two mile long road, lined with beeches, to Carruchan. Fine views over Dumfries to the north are obtained on the way. The road finally bends left and joins the Dalbeattie Road (A711) at Drumsleet. Turn left along this for half a mile to where the Moss Road goes off on the left. The Moss Road passes through old woods and then a flat valley back to the starting point in about two miles. Distance, 6 miles.

5 Brownrigg, Heathall, Marchfield, Brownrigg TPRPRC

Leave the Lockerbie Road (A709) by a grassy track on the north side, almost opposite the entrance to Brownrigg Loaning (996 771). After half a mile the track becomes a path, curving right, then left and winding through the woods, finally going along the side of a sawmill and coming to a road at the old railway bridge (991 789). A turn sharp left here brings the walker to the Moffat Road (A701) at The Grove. Turn left towards Dumfries and in ½ mile turn left again into a path that starts at a gap in the sandstone wall just before

Path down the Nith from Kingholm

Marchfield House. This path goes across to Summerfield Farm and from there by a road back to the Lockerbie Road at Clumpton, a few hundred yards from the start at Brownrigg. Distance, about 3½ miles. At Heathhall, instead of going on to the Moffat Road a descent may be made at the railway bridge on to the course of the railway and this followed for the half mile to the path from Marchfield to Summerfield.

6 Douievale to Barton's House RPC

This short walk leaves the Annan Road (A75) at Douievale (010 760) about 2½ miles out. Follow the tarred road to the last house and go past this on its left. A path goes on through the wood and over fields arriving at the Lockerbie Road (A709) near Barton's House, after some 20 minutes walking. Another 20 minutes takes you back to the starting point. If desired, a round walk may be made by turning right along the Lockerbie Road after Barton's House and then right again after half a mile. Another mile brings you to Collin, a mile along the Annan Road from the start at Douievale. Distances: Barton's House and back, about 2½ miles. Round by Collin, about 4 miles. The new Dumfries by-pass may alter the layout here.

7 Kingholm Quay, Camp Hill, Maidenbower, Kingholm PTPRPRC

Kingholm Quay lies on the river bank some 2 miles down from the town centre, and a car may conveniently be left here. Follow the path that goes down the river bank for about a mile, to where a lane from Netherwood Mains meets it. Go up this lane, through the farm, cross the Glencaple Road and continue uphill, keeping to the left of Netherwood Bank. At a stile on the crest of the hill it is worth turning right to the little chump of trees on the round summit of Camp Hill (312ft) from where a very fine view is obtainable. Go down the few remaining yards to the Bankend Road, turn right and in a few yards a footpath on the left goes down past Hightown to Craigs Road. Turn left again and in about a mile the sandstone conglomerate cliff of Mid Craigs is seen on the left. After another half mile, at the roadend to Maidenbower House, a footpath goes straight up to the base of the Maidenbower Craigs, another section of sandstone cliffs, cut up by some steep gullies. The footpath can be followed to the top of the crags at either end or by some scrambling in between. On the top a gate indicates where a path leads down past Midpark Farm to the Bankend Road again. If a passage through the hospital grounds is permissible, this brings you to the end of Kingholm Loaning and so back to Kingholm Quay; if not, a detour of half a mile outwards to Stone house Loaning should be made, then back along the Bankend Road to the top of Kingholm Loaning. Total distance, about 6½ miles.

8   Lennox Tower (933727)

This well preserved cylindrical stone tower of granite blocks was built by the Lennox family some 200 years ago as a garden folly, when the hillside was bare. It has a sandstone plaque with the Lennox crest, a lion rampant, above the entrance door. It stands high on the hillside above Dalskairth and is marked on the old 2½ inch Ordnance maps. It is difficult to find and to reach. The best approach is from the track leading from Lochanhead to Hillhead Farm. Before reaching the farm head along the stone dyke for the clump of trees on the left and keep round it to the left near the top. It is difficult to see the tower until one is at it because of the thick trees and rhododendrons. There is no path, but there is talk of one being made. Distance about ½ mile from the track.

9   Terregles, Collochan, Seeside, Terregles   RC

A car may be left near Terregles school (Bowhouse) at (931 771). The narrow country road is followed uphill for rather less than ½ mile. Go past the first fork and at the second go to the right. Follow this road uphill, past Collochan Farm and then, on the right, its little loch. Continue uphill, then down, in ½ mile, to a T-junction. Turn right and pass Seeside, continuing past another road from the left and then downhill. In about a mile, downhill, passing the entrance to The Grove, a return is made to Terregles. Distance, 4 miles.

10   Newbridge, Cluden Path to Irongray, Newbridge   PRC

Newbridge may be reached by bus, and a car may be left in the side road near the bridge, 3 miles from Dumfries on the A76 road to Kilmarnock. Cross the bridge and descend immediately to the river bank. There used to be good stone steps down the side of the bridge, but some of these have been damaged and it may be necessary to go round the corner and through a gate to get down. The path goes along the river bank to the Mill at East Cluden. The path is in bad condition and has fallen into the river in parts — considerable care is needed if the river is high. Continue from the Mill along the river's edge, and again care is needed. After ½ mile the valley widens and the going becomes easier towards the bridge, and then left again down the road on the south side of the Cluden for some 2 miles. Turn sharp left again for Newbridge. Alternatively, at the bridge at Irongray turn right for ½ mile and then right again and return to Newbridge by the Gribton road on the north side of the Cluden. Distance, either way, about 5 miles. This walk up the Cluden is always picturesque, and when the river is high, spectacular.

11   Glencaple, Kelton Cove, Kelton, Glencaple   RPRC

Bus or car may be used to get to Glencaple, 6 miles downstream from Dumfries on (B725). A side road goes off uphill past the school for a straight mile and a half towards the War Memorial on the Bankend Road. Turn left there and go north for nearly two miles with good views on both sides. Here, at a house on the left (005 719) is the start of a right-of-way path across the hill to Kelton. The path dips and rises again. A few hundred yards to the right, after the dip, is a small sandstone escarpment. This has in it two small caves, linked by a low arch, and these are easily visited. Returning from the caves to the path, the mile downhill to Kelton gives good views across the Nith. Turn left to return to Glencaple. Distance, about 6 miles.

12   Collin, Torthwald Castle, Collin   RC

By car or bus to Collin on the Annan Road (A75). Coming from Dumfries turn into the first road on the left at Collin and a mile's walk brings you to the Lockerbie Road (A709). Turn right, for ½ mile, then right again past the old, not very picturesque castle. After ¼ mile fork right for a road back to Collin, giving a short round of about 3 miles. For longer rounds, continue for another mile before turning right for Collin (4 miles), or for a further mile to West Mains before coming down to the Annan Road and then Collin (5 miles). The Dumfries by-pass may alter the start.

13   Ellisland Farm

Home for a time of Rober Burns, this farm is one of the places of pilgrimage for Burns' enthusiasts. It lies a quarter of a mile east of the main A76 road to Kilmarnock, about 6 miles north of Dumfries. Car or bus may be taken to the roadend at (926 837) and the short track walked down to the buildings and the nearby river. The farm, now in the hands of a trust, is open to the public. Distance down and back, about ½ mile.

14   Terregles, Irongray, Nunwood, Terregles   RC

The cross roads at Terregles (Bownhouse) (931 774) may be reached by car, some 3 miles from Dumfries. Walk for ½ mile towards The Grove and just before it turn right, up and over by a quiet narrow road to Irongray Church. Here turn right for 1½ miles to Nunwood junction (945 789). Turn right again and another 1½ miles brings you back to Terregles crossroads. Distance, 4½ miles.

Terregles Woods

15   Lochrutton (Lochfoot), Kirkgate, Overbanks, Lochfoot
RPRC

Car or bus to Lochfoot. Walk ½ mile towards Dumfries along Old Military Road. Turn right at Longrutton Gate and after Lochrutton Church turn left along footpath beside wall. This brings you down after about 1 mile to the Old Military Road and left again to return to Lochfoot (4 miles).

16   Greenmerse   RNC

Car or bus down New Abbey Road to (959 711), opposite the end of the Moss Road. Walk down (1½ miles) to Greenmerse Farm, past it on the left down a muddy track to the dyke on the Green Merse. The dyke can be followed for short distances to left or right, or in dry conditions the merse can be walked over to the Nith. An excellent short walk to see many birds, but can be muddy (3-4 miles). Return to starting point.

17   Up the Cargen Water   PRC

Go out the Castle-Douglas Road for about a mile. Go under the railway bridge and cross the over the Cargen a few yards farther on. Here turn down to the river bank and follow the path upstream — a delightful walk and a right-of-way. But it is better to go in dry conditions. The path continues for some two miles to the bridge at Waterside (929 757). Here turn right for 1½ miles to the crossroads at Terregles, turn right again for some 3 miles back to the centre of Dumfries; or at the old Maxwelltown station turn right again for ½ mile back to the starting bridge over the Cargen.

Distances: Round walk from Dumfries, about 7 miles; round from the bridge over the Cargen, 5 miles. The new Dumfries by-pass may alter the layout at the start.

SECTION 2
The region between the New Abbey Road A710, the Dalbeattie Road A711 and the coast

1 Mabie and adjoining forests

Most of the ground in the triangle formed by the Dalbeattie Road, Moss Road and New Abbey Road, Beeswing - New Abbey Road, is now under forest. The section north of the track from Whinnyhill to Lochanhead is Mabie Forest. The southern section still has a few unforested patches and has no single name. There is a narrow public road from Whinnyhill by Troston to Glensone and this gives access to some walks. Other access routes are as follows:

(i)   Moss Road (951 721). Track slopes up to right and comes to an end above Dalskairth after about 1 mile. But footpaths can be found leading to other tracks at a higher level.

(ii)   Moss Road (955 716). Track through Burnside Farm, various branches.

(iii   Mabie Lodge on New Abbey Road (955 707). Road to Mabie House Hotel. Several branches from there, now signposted, with notes available from the Forestry Commission. mission.

(iv)   Road to Butterhole and Mabie House from half mile further up the New Abbey Road (959 702).

(v)   Whinnyhill (963 688). Road to Troston can be followed by car through to Glensone on Beeswing Road. Access to forest from it may be had from several points. From junction after 1½ miles, turn right towards Craigbill Farm then left and straight on. This track leads through to Lochanhead.

(vi)   Continue on Troston Road for another half mile. Track on right leads to Craigend (ruins) and through by path (often wet and muddy) to Moorend on Dalbeattie Road, or by Lochbank Hill through to cottages near Cairnyard on Dalbeattie Road (905 703).

(vii)   Lochanlead. Road to Woodhead Farm. Turn sharp left before farm, then sharp right after ¼ mile. This is start of the direct track through to Mabie House (iii) and is about 3¼ miles direct.

(viii) As (vii), but after ¼ mile mentioned continue straight on, branching right before Hillhead Farm. This track winds round and can lead to Burnside (ii) or Mabie Hotel (iii).

(ix) Dalbeattie Road. At the foot of the long straight part of the Long Wood a path goes uphill to the left to Hillhead Farm and can be used to join (viii).

GENERAL. There are many side tracks that can be taken to give longer or shorter walks from the above access points. One specially worth trying is from the highest point of the route (vii) — turn left then after half mile right and follow track to look-out at top of Marthrown Hill. This is a fine viewpoint.

Adjoining forests

(x) From (vi) take track on left of Troston road instead of right. This goes round Troston Hill and a route (no path part of way; very rough) can be made through to the Auchengray Plantation and the Beeswing Road near Mossyard.

(xi) From cottages (vi) on Dalbeattie Road (905 703) various tracks branch. One goes through to Lochbank Hill to (vi). Another, lower track, can be followed to emerge at Low Lochbank on the Beeswing Road.

2 Round Marthrown Hill   TC

The starting point of this walk through Mabie Forest can be at Burnside (953 713), which may be reached by car from the New Abbey Road (bus to roadend). A car may be left there. A track goes sharply uphill on the right into the trees above, where it meets a forest track. Turn left and follow this track to the Marthrown of Mabie House, at which good views are obtained. Turn right here up a grassy track and then down past the ruined Marthrown of Woodhead. Continue until the farm track to Hillhead is joined, keeping left, above and parallel to the Dalbeattie Road at the Long Wood. At a junction, with a new house, (918 718) turn left and go past Lochaber Cottage. At the next fork take the left branch uphill and continue on the main track over the summit, eastwards. In about ½ mile go past a side track on the left, and then shortly fork left at (941 707), keeping to the left side of the burn. At a 4-cross road go straight on, downhill back to Burnside. This route is shown by dotted lines on the 1:50,000 O.S. map, but is not easy to see on it, and with so many forest tracks care is needed to follow the correct route. Distance, about 6 miles. This round walk might equally well start at the new house mentioned, above Lochanhead. (See (vii) in No 1.)

3 Whinnyhill, Troston, Glensone, New Abbey, Whinnyhill   RC

Go by car or bus down the New Abbey Road (A710) just past the summit at Whinnyhill, where a road goes off to the right. A car may be left about here. Walk up this road for some two miles, then down to Troston and Glensone. Turn left and go down the picturesque road towards New Abbey, in about 3 miles. The village and Sweetheart Abbey may be visited from here. Otherwise turn left again and go up the main road, through the avenue of splendid trees of Shambellie Wood, and in about a mile and a half return to the starting point. Distance, about 8 miles.

4 New Abbey, by Kirkconnell   RC

Out by New Abbey Road for 4½ miles to foot of the big rise at Whinnyhill (959 704). Here you will see a 'lodge' on the left, with a gate as at a private avenue; but this road is really public. Turn into it and you will have a delightful walk by woods and under huge oak

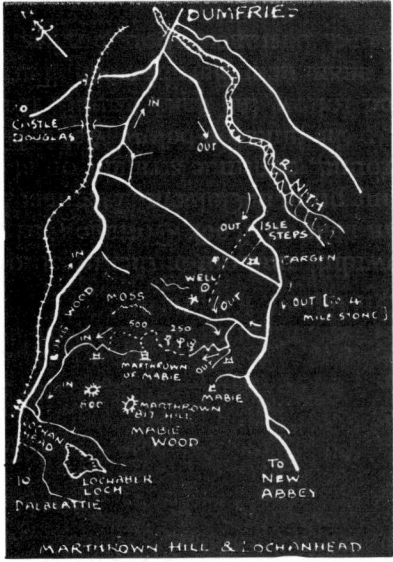

trees, till you reach the gates at Kirkconnell House, when the road swings sharp right and begins a series of switchback ups and downs, being some of the very steepest hills on any road about here. You soon get fine vistas of the Solway, and later of Loch Kindar, Sweetheart Abbey, Criffell, and Shambellie woods; a perfect picture, hard to beat anywhere. After rejoining the New Abbey Road turn right and return over Whinnyhill, in about 2½ miles to the starting point. Distance, about 5 miles.

5   Kirkconnell - New Abbey by river banks   PNRC

Car to corner near Kirkconnell House (979 681). Follow track to left to Mains cottage. Turn right along faint track at edge of wood. This track goes on and out of the wood, and can be very muddy, but contractors for a drainage scheme have made a road here for about a mile. It becomes a footpath and continues past Airds Point and up the right bank of the New Abbey Burn for about 1 mile. A path to the right leads up to Airds Farm and a return can be made to the starting point by the road (5-6 miles). Or the burn may be crossed by footbridge (978 663) to left and return made by Maryfield and Shambellie Grange (6-7 miles). Or, after Maryfield turn left again and cross by bridge to footpath round the walls of Sweetheart Abbey and return through New Abbey and Shambellie Grange. This extends the walk to some 7-8 miles.

6   Lotus Hill   N*

Coming from Beeswing, leave the road at a gate on the right just before the descent to Loch Arthur (895 688). Aim for the right-hand side of the trees and continue beyond them to the top (1056 feet). The going is rough and wet. A descent can be made very steeply towards Glensone, and return by the road to the stating point (3-4 miles).

7   Kinharvie Burn   RT

From the Kinharvie roadend (926 670) a road goes round the back of the houses and is succeeded by a track on the west side of the Kinharvie Burn. The burn is very picturesque, with pools and gullies and fine trees. The track continues for some 2 miles. Shortly before it ends on the moor it is crossed at right angles by a recent forestry track. This goes a short distance west towards Lotus Hill on one side. On the other, east side, it crosses the burn and meets a recent extension of the track from the Solway Fisheries (No 8) round the hillside above Kinharvie. This extension continues south past the junction for another half mile to the open moor. Hence No 7 may be finished by using No 8 for a return or vice versa. Distance, Kinharvie to end of track, about 2 miles. Round trip of No 7 and No 8, about 6 miles.

8 Tannock Burn T

Leave Beeswing-New Abbey Road by road to the Solway Fishery (939 665), and turn right into the forest. The track branches immediately, the right branch going towards Kinharvie and this may, with some difficulty, be linked with the track in 7 above. The left branch goes up the hillside above the Fishery and follows the line of the Tannock Burn on to Craig Moss where it stops at the end of the forest. A return may be made over Tannock Hill to Kinharvie, or down the Glen Burn to New Abbey; both rough going. Where this track crosses the Tannock Burn (944 658) a branch to the right winds up on to the slope of Tannock Hill and stops; this point gives good views. Distances to ends of tracks, about 2 miles each way.

9 New Abbey to Boreland of Southwick PNP(X)

Leave New Abbey by the road to Glen Farm and the Waterloo Monument. Cross the burn by the footbridge before the farm and follow the burn for some 2 miles. Then cross burn to the right side and aim south-west for the slight dip between Meikle Hard Hill and Boreland Hill. Over the dip, the Mid Burn leads down to Boreland of Southwick (5 miles). Another $2\frac{1}{2}$ miles takes you to the coast road at Caulkerbush.

10 Shore walk RNRC

Walk from Kirkbean to Carsethorn, then to right along shore past Borron Point and Arbigland to Powillimount. Half a mile up from Powillimount turn right and follow a road back to Kirkbean. Some parts of the shore are very rough, but the views on a good day are excellent. (6-7 miles.)

11   Redbank Hill   TC

Leave the coast road at the old lodge for Southwick House at a left-hand corner (939 570) and follow the track uphill. Take the right branch at each fork and wind up the side of Redbank Hill. After the summit between Redbank Hill and Airdrie Hill the road forks. Both branches continue until near the north-west edge of the forest. Return by the same road. Out and back, about 5 miles.

A very rough round may be made by going through from either of the last branches to the open moor below Bail Fell, down the edge of the forest and back along the bottom, but the going is very rough.

12   Woodside Hill   TC

Half a mile up the Caulkerbush-Dalbeattie Road turn right. Just after the bridge at Woodside a track inclines up to the left. This leads round the north end of the wooded hill into the secluded glen between Woodside Hill and Redbank Hill, and can be followed past a ruined cottage back to the starting point (2 miles from Woodside). Or, at the ruined cottage, a route may be made (very rough) across the valley to the track of No 11, emerging at the lodge on the coast road. This makes a round of 5-6 miles.

13   Dalbeattie Forest   T

Entrances to the forest can be made from roadends at:

(i)	Cloak Moss (858 594)	(v)	Auchensheen (852 555)
(ii)	Near Auchenbay (874 576)	(vi)	Woodside (840 572)
(iii)	Drumburn (883 548)	(vii)	Little Righorn (836 596)
(iv)	Lochend (868 545)	(viii)	Dalbeattie (838 606)

Tracks from these lead round and across the forest. Through or circular routes may be made. From (viii) an attractive lochan in the trees is only some half mile from the town. (The Plantain Loch).

14   Southwick Halt   RTR

Car to road junction near Loch Fern (865 629). Take road down to right towards the (derelict) Southwick Halt. At old railway track turn left. A track leads round the hillside and up to Barclosh Farm, then rejoins the road. Turn left to return to Loch Fern and junction (3 miles).

15 Round Fell and Maidenpap NC*

Leave the back road from Kirkgunzeon to Caulkerbush at about (890 603) where a track goes off, signposted to 'Gliding Club'. Leave this track at a convenient point and go up the slopes of Round Fell and then onto Maidenpap. The ground is now forested and the going is very rough. On the top of Maidenpap, 1032 feet, is an old stone shooting box. There is a fine extensive view. Distance, about 2½ miles.

16 Caulkerbush (Southwick), Auchenskeoch, Clifton Crags RC

Go by car or bus to the bridge and War Memorial at Caulkerbush (Southwick) junction (928 572). From here walk up the road to Dalbeattie (A745) through the attractive Southwick glen for some three miles. Half a mile past Auchenskeoch take the road on the left and follow it down the glen of the Back Burn. The road passes the ruins of the pre-Reformation Southwick Old Church and its churchyard on one side and cliffs of Clifton Crags on the other side, and comes down to the coast road. Turn left to return to the starting point. There is some rock scrambling to be had on Clifton Crags. Distance, 6 miles.

17 Caulkerbush, Doonside, Sandyhills, Caulkerbush RC

From the same starting point as No 16 this gives a longer round. Go as in No 16 from the Southwick Bridge up the Dalbeattie Road for 3½ miles before turning left. The road winds southwards past Drumstinchall and Doonside and the old farmhouse of Fairgirth on the right. This last incorporates the remains of the old chapel of Saint Lawrence. The road reaches the coast at Sandyhills. Here turn left for 3 miles up, down and along the Heughs back to Southwick Distance, about 9 miles.

18 Auchenskeoch, Clonyard, New Farm RTR

A car may be left near the junction on the Dalbeattie to Caulkerbush road (B793) just below Auchenskeoch. Continue on the road eastwards for some ½ mile and turn off right on a farm track. This leads down and over the Caulkerbush Burn then up to Clonyard. Turn right here and follow the road past New Farm and round left to the back road from Upper Clifton. Turn right and go north for ½ mile to the B793 again, then right again back to the start. Distance, 4 miles.

19   Sandyhills to Portling   (i) NPRC   (ii) NRC

Go by car or bus to Sandyhills and go down the lane to the sands. Turn right along the beach and cross the burn by the footbridge, if available, and then cross the track from Douglas Hall. If the footbridge is gone, go round by Douglas Hall.

(i) By the cliff path. Go up a path on the right that keeps close to the edge of the cliffs along the side of the fields. At one point you can see down through the natural rock arch on the shore below. The path goes over a stile to the road at Portling. Turn right uphill, then right again at the top of the hill for $\frac{1}{2}$ mile to the main road and right again to return to the start at Sandyhills. Distance, about 3 miles.

(ii) By the shore. This shore route should only be attempted when the tide is full out, and even then you will probably get wet feet. After crossing the footbridge, turn left down to an attractive small sandy bay. Go to the right, keeping to the sand near the edge of the rocks. Usually this sand is firm, but there may be some shallow pools which are skirted on the left. There are several caves, one long, narrow and dark, and one spectacular rock arch. At Portling go up from the shore to join the road as in (i). Distance about the same.

20   Portling, Cliff Path, Castle Point, Rockliffe   PNRC

A car may be left where the road starts to descend steeply to Portling. Walk the last half mile of rough road to Port o'Warren. Here the cliff path goes off uphill steeply on the right, just before the track continues to the houses on the shore. The cliff path goes high above the sea with fine views of the cliffs and the sea birds. There are many interesting rock formations on the way to Castle Point, especially at Gutcher's Isle. If the tide is out the sandy shore may be followed to Castle Point instead of the cliff path. There is now a continuous, marked path all the way from Sandyhills or Douglas Hall to Rockliffe. A bus on the A710 may aid the return to Sandyhills or Portling. Distance on path, about 4 miles. P.

21   Colvend, Barnbarroch, Colvend, forest walk   TPTRC

At a bend in the road at Colvend where a side road goes off on the north side (868 546) a car may be left. Go by this side road up the east side of the White Loch and fork left after Lochside by a path that goes along the east side of Barean Loch to a 4-way junction (858

Barcloy Hill towards Rockcliffe

Solway Sands to Portling

563). Turn left downhill, and out of the forest to Auchensheen and return to the main road at Rock Cottage (851 555). Turn left to return to the starting point at Colvend. Distance, about 3 miles. For a slightly longer round, continue straight on at the 4-junction for another half mile to the junction below Moyle Hill (851 572). Turn sharp left here and follow the track round, near the edge of the forest, to the road again near Barnbarroch. Turn left again for 2½ miles back to Colvend. Distance, about 6 miles.

22   Kippford, Jubilee Path, Rockcliffe, Kippford
RPRC or RPRPC

Kippford may be reached by car or bus. At the Post Office go steeply uphill to the left and follow the attractive 'Jubilee Path' which leads in about 1½ miles to Rockliffe. A return may be made to Kippford by the sam attractive route, but a different route may be tried. At the end of the straight piece of road from Rockliffe past Barons Craig go on into the forest instead of turning left along the Jubilee Path. Take the left fork at each of the next two, and either at the third. These tracks stop at the edge of the trees in rather less than a mile, and the same, steep path goes left from them downhill into Kippford. Distance by alternative route, 3½ miles.

Causeway to Rough Island, Kippford

23   Barnbarroch, along the Urr, Kippford   PRC

On the road from Dalbeattie to Kippford it is possible to leave a car somewhere about the roadend to Upper Barnbarroch (840 572). A short distance farther on, a side road on the right goes down to a cottage and a path from there take you down to the river bank. There is a footpath along the bank for most of the way, but there are occasional gaps, and if the river is, or has recently been, high there are some wet and muddy sections before the boat-slips at Kippford are reached. Here turn left uphill, then left again to return to the starting point of the walk. Distance, about 2½ miles.

Solway Sands, Sandyhills Bay

24   Criffell, 1868ft   *

Looking north from the Cumberland coast Criffell is conspicuous on the Solway coast opposite; coming west from Carlisle it is prominent on the skyline; from Dumfries it can be seen clearly to the south, and from far along the Solway coast to the west it is the highest point to be seen to the east. Although it is only 1868 feet high, it is isolated and hence, as well as being visible from all sides, it is itself an unusually fine viewpoint. From its summit can be seen the

Moffat hills, some of the Cheviots, the northern Pennines, the hills of the Lake District, the Isle of Man, the Galloway hills, the Lowther hills, and through a gap to the north-west Goat Fell and The Castles in Arran, some 80 miles away. Its ascent, in varying weather, is very rewarding, whether for the distant views or for the more local panorama of Solway sandbanks and channels. Because of its situation the weather on it can change very quickly, and mist can come down quite suddenly. The hill is made of granite, is steep and very rough in parts, and some of the slopes are now planted with trees. For the ascent, boots should be worn, and a map and compass carried. There is a variety of routes to the summit and approximate distances and times are given below. Times vary greatly according to individuals and an average figure is suggested.

(i) From ARDWALL. Leave the New Abbey Road (A710) by the side road at (979 639) to Ardwall. Cars should be left before reaching the farm. A track to the left, then right, is signposted to Criffell. The track goes up a forestry ride beside a burn and over a stile on to the moor. From here the path goes up diagonally to the left through the heather directly to the top. Distance from Ardwall to the top, about $1\frac{1}{2}$ miles. Time, about $1\frac{1}{2}$ hours up, 1 hour down.

(ii) Also from ARDWALL. At the stile in (i), continue straight on to the col (lowest point) in the ridge coming from Knockendoch, the smaller pointed hill on the right. Turn left at the ridge and go along it to the top. Distances and time as in (i)

(iii) From KIRKBEAN. Go up the path, now very overgrown with gorse and brambles, on the right (north) side of the burn for about a mile and so on to the south shoulder of the hill. Continue up its rounded slopes to the top. Distance, about $2\frac{1}{2}$ miles. Time, 2 hours up, $1\frac{1}{2}$ hours down. The most direct route from Kirkbean is by the road past Criffell House, leaving the main road $\frac{1}{2}$ mile north of the village.

(iv) From SOUTHWICK. From the bridge at Southwick go along the Dalbeattie Road (B793) for $\frac{1}{2}$ mile and fork right. Follow this road for $1\frac{1}{2}$ miles to a narrow, sharp bridge corner just before Boreland of Southwick. A car may be left near here. Walk up the track past the farm and, before crossing the burn, turn up right (east) on to the slopes of Boreland Hill. From there a small dip and then a final rise, in a north-easterly direction, takes you to the summit of

Criffell. Distance from bridge mentioned, about 3 miles. Time, 2½ hours up, 2 hours down.

(v) From DRUMBURN. Leave the New Abbey Road at Drumburn (980 621) and go up the side road for about ½ mile until it is possible to see a gap in the line of trees above, on the slopes of Criffell. Make for this gap and continue more or less straight up the steep slopes to the top. This is the steepest route up and down. Distance, 1½ miles. Time, 1½ hours up, 1 hour down.

(vi) From NEW ABBEY. Two slightly different routes are possible. For both, leave the 'square' at New Abbey by the road that twists up to Glen Farm and the Waterloo Monument. Just before the farm go left by the footbridge over the burn.

(a) By the Glen Burn. Follow the footpath up the east side of the burn for about two miles, to where the burn forks. Keep beside the left fork that goes up in the direction of the summit and continue to the top.

(b) By Knockendoch. About ½ mile up from the footbridge in (a) go up left on to the crest of the long ridge coming down from Knockendoch and follow this to the summit of Knockendoch. Continue along this ridge, a little downhill at first to the south-west and then up, south at first then south-east to the summit of Criffell.

Distance either way, about 3 miles. Time, 2½ hours up, 2 hours down.

By arranging transport to suit, by car or bus, it is possible to go up by one route and down by another, giving views of the hill from two different aspects.

25 Plascow Moor   RTC

Turn off the Dalbeattie Road (A711) to the left at the crossroads near Kirkgunzeon (872 663) and again left almost immediately into a narrow road. After ½ mile the road forks and a car may be left here on the grass verge. Take the right fork and in ½ mile fork left towards the trees. The track goes along the side of the trees for about a mile and then goes on to the moor, up past a small sandpit and a ruined cottage to end on the moor. It would be possible to continue over the moor and descend to Boreland of Southwick, and there are signs that the forestry track could be so extedned. The present end of the track gives good open views to the north-west. A return is made by the same route. Distance, about 4 miles.

Hauf Netters at Kippford

26 Rose Cottage Walks

These start from the cottage mentioned in Section 2, I, VI and XI at (905 703) on A711 and give access to the south part of Mabie Forest. After a quarter of a mile the track branches in to three. The right hand branch is the first to be reached from Rose Cottage and it turns sharply downhill, then curves left above Loch Arthur and soon comes to the edge of the plantation. From here a short distance on grass takes you to the track from Lochbank Farm down to Beeswing road. Turn right along the road to Beeswing, right again at Beeswing and follow the A711 back to the start. About 4 miles. TNRC

The middle branch turns off right soon after the right hand branch and goes on almost parallel and slightly above it to the edge of the plantation. The rest of the route is as already described. About 4 miles. TNRC

The left hand branch goes uphill, then down and then curves round Lochbank Hill and continues downhill to the junction at (933 692) on the Troston road. A return can be made the same way. Distance each way, about 2 miles.   T

27   Southwick Merse

Many people consider that the stretch of sand that runs 5 or 6 miles west form Southerness to opposite Sandyhills is the finest in the district. Unfortunately it is not possible to reach it directly from Sandyhills as the Southwick Burn, which is deep and can be dangerous, intervenes, and it is five miles each way from the other end at Southerness. It is possible to reach the best parts by following a track that records show has been used for many years. From the War Memorial at Caulkerbush (No 16) go east along the A711 for some 200 yards and turn right down a straight tarred road for a quarter of a mile to Beck's Bridge, and on for another quarter mile to Croftfoot Corner where a gate leads to a grassy track that takes you past a corner (918 557) on to the open merse. Straight ahead is the big Mersehead sandbank with its line of white shells. Veering left takes you round the corner to face Southerness, and here traces of sea coal may often be found. Veering right at the corner takes you over the grass to the Southwick Burn nearly opposite the Needle's Eye, but do not attempt to cross it. There is a difference of opinion as to whether the final part of the track is a public path. RTN. Distance from Caulkerbush to sandbank, about 2 miles each way.

28   Shambellie Round

This is a picturesque short walk mainly on forestry tracks, round Shambellie Wood. A car may be left at New Abbey. Walk up through the old Shambellie pines on the Dumfries road for half a mile and turn left to West Shambellie. Continue on the forest track past it. This winds through the trees above the Mark Burn and after a mile or so curves round at the top of the hill to give good views of Criffell and Loch Kindar. It then dips down again through the trees to reach the Beeswing - New Abbey Road a mile west of New Abbey and so back to the start. RTC. Distance about 4 miles.

29   Round Duff's Loch

This attractive small loch is less than a quarter of a mile from the A710 from Dalbeattie to Colvend but is barely visible from it. There is a convenient lay-by on the west side of A710 about 4 miles from Dalbeattie to leave a car. Walk on uphill to the turn-off to the east at Rock Cottage. Follow this side road downhill and fork left after half a mile, past the long grasses at the water's edge. A track with a stile leads along the lochside for a quarter of a mile and crosses a field to reach the road to Loch House. Turn left on this road back to the A710 about ½ mile from the start. RPNRC Distance about 2½ miles.

30 New Abbey-West Glen Circuit RPR

The construction of a new forestry road has made possible this attractive circuit with good views to Loch Kindar and the Solway beyond.

A car may be left at New Abbey, or New Abbey may be reached by local bus. Take the side road past the Corn Mill towards the Waterloo Monument. At the end of the tarred road, after about a mile, is a Water Department cottage at the start of the track to the Waterloo Monument. Turn left here over a wooden footbridge. Follow the track past a cottage, uphill, to a stile on to a rough forestry track. Follow this track for another ½ mile to where it joins the new forestry road. If a longer walk is desired, this road continues uphill for another mile or so and stops. If not, turn left, downhill, at the junction. The forestry road meanders downhill through the trees, fields and finally houses to regain the A710 at the petrol station in New Abbey. Turn left back to the centre of New Abbey. Distance about 4 miles, mostly on road.

SECTION 3
Region between the Dalbeattie Road A711 and the Castle-Douglas Road A75

The quiet side roads in this region give pleasant road walks.

1 Under the Brae RTPRC

Leave car at first junction (886 734) beyond Lochfoot on the Old Military Road and turn left downhill. After about 2 miles turn right along track to Abune the Brae. A path then continues across the Under Brae Lane — soft going to the Old Road again at Gateside. Return by road. (5 miles.)

2 Milton to Beeswing RPR(X)

From Milton Crossroads take first turning on right going towards Dumfies. This leads to Crochmore from where a good path leads over the hillside to Lawston and then the road to Beeswing. (4 miles.)

3   Kirkgunzeon, Cowar, Kirgunzeon   RC

Leave car at Kirkgunzeon and follow Milton Road for half a mile. Take the left fork past Killymingan. The road winds on to Alleyford from where a short track links with the road at Little Cocklick. At the next junction turn left past Cowar and Porterbelly to the Dalbeattie Road and so return to Kirkgunzeon. (6 miles.)

4   Milton Loch   RC

Leave car at junction at Auchengibbert (832 714). Take road to left past Milton Loch to Milton. Turn right along Old Military Road for $2\frac{1}{2}$ miles and right again past Crofthaed and back to Auchengibbert. ($6\frac{1}{2}$ miles.)

A shorter round can be made by turning right at Lochside up a rough track which goes past a quarry on Fell Hill and rejoins the road. Turn right for Auchengibbert (2 miles); or go straight on along an attractive grassy path which can be followed as far as Springholm on the Castle-Douglas Road.

5   Mote of Urr   PRTRPC

A car may be left at Netheryett on the road from Dalbeattie to Haugh of Urr (A719) (818 647). Cross the river by the footbridge just below the ford. (Do not try to take a car across the ford!) The Mote of Urr is immediately up on the right. Go on up the road and under the old railway track and take the first fork to the left to East Logan. Turn left again here and go down the track to the course of the railway. Here turn left and go along the track back to the road you came up from the footbridge, and so back to Netheryett. Distance, about 3 miles. It may be possible to cross the burn going into the Urr at the foot of the track from East Logan and return to the footbridge along the bank of the Urr; this will depend on the water conditions.

6   Milton of Buittle   RT

Turn off the Castle-Douglas Road (A75) to the left half-way up the hill from the Urr Bridge (783 654). Cross the Old Military Road and take left fork. Leave car where the road crosses the old railway track. Walk downhill, turn left and follow road up and down hill to Milton of Buittle. This gives a very picturesque and overall view of the Mote of Urr. Return to car by using the old railway track. (3-4 miles.)

7   Urr Valley   TPTC

On the road from Dalbeattie to Castle-Douglas (A745) about halfway up Buittle Hill a narrow road goes down right here. Walk down the road past Buittle Place and take the left fork uphill. The track goes through a picturesque defile to Barrsyard and continues in a north-west direction, rather faintly in parts, for $\frac{1}{2}$ mile to meet the road, near East Logan. Turn right and go downhill to the course of the old railway. Turn right and go along the track to just before the site of the old railway bridge. A path will be seen here going along the edge of the wood back towards Buittle Place, and then a track back to the start. Distance, about 4 miles.

8   Buittle Reservoir   RPRC

Go along the Dalbeattie—Castle-Douglas Road (A745) to the crossroads at Buittle Church (807 602). A car may be left about here. Walk along the narrow road on the right (north) side for about a mile, when a small reservoir is seen below to the right. A path goes down from the roadside along the north side of this reservoir and down, fairly steeply, to the farm road to Buittle Mains. Continue down to the main road and turn right back to the starting place. Distance, about 3 miles.

9   Buittle, West and East Logan, Buittle   RTRC

This is a slightly longer walk from the same starting place as No. 8 and combining part of No. 7. Go past the reservoir of No. 8 for a total of 2 miles from the start until a 'T' junction is reached. Turn right here and very shortly fork right by the road leading to West Logan. Go past West Logan and shortly turn right to East Logan. Just before East Logan turn right on to the path that crosses over, faintly, to Barrsyard (see No. 7). Continue by the track south past Buittle Place back to the main road and go to the right for about a mile back to the starting place. Distance, about $5\frac{1}{2}$ miles.

10   Lochanhead, Mains of Hills, Lochfoot, Lochanhead   PRC

Go out the Dalbeattie Road (A711) to Lochanhead (916 717), where a car may be left. Cross the bridge over the old railway line and immediately go through a gate on the right. Turn left by a path that goes up just outside the grounds of the adjacent house. The path curves over the hillside and down to Mains of Hills, and its old tower, passing along their east sides and continuing northwards over the next hill slope. At Lochrutton Church turn left down to the Old Military Road, and left again there for ½ mile to the Lochfoot crossroads. There turn left for some 2 miles back by the road to Lochanhead. Distance, about 5 miles.

11 Beeswing, Lochrutton, Lochanhead, Beeswing RC

A car may be left at Beeswing on the Dalbeattie Road (A711). Turn right at the crossroads at the church and go over the old rail line uphill, curving round and coming down towards Lochrutton after 2½ miles. In another ½ mile turn right down to Lochfoot, then right again for 2 miles over, as in No. 10, to Lochanhead. Here turn right again for 2 miles back to Beeswing. Distance, about 8 miles.

12 Drumcoltran Tower, Kirkgunzeon RC or RTC

About a mile past Beeswing on the Dalbeattie Road (A745) a road goes off on the right (886 684). A car may be left about here. The road crosses the old rail line and turns left before Blairshinnoch. In another mile Drumcoltran is reached with its historic old tower. In another ½ mile turn left down to Kirkgunzeon. There turn left again and go through the village, forking left at the junction at the top of the little hill. This takes you in about ½ mile back to the Dalbeattie Road, and going left for a mile brings you back to the start. To avoid the mile along the busy road it is possible to go back along the old rail track, but do not go on to it until you have crossed the burn where the rail track goes over it. Distance, about 5 miles.

13 Haugh of Urr, Redcastle, Moss Side, Haugh of Urr RPRC

Haugh of Urr on the B794 road may be reached from Dalbeattie or from the A75 Castle-Douglas road, and a car left there. Going towards Dalbeattie, at the south end of the village where the main road forks right, go straight on for ½ mile, past the church and turn left to Redcastle. A track goes on over the hill in a direction a little north of east, becoming a path and going down to Moss Side in about a mile from Redcastle. Turn left at the roadend and, in 1½ miles, at tne Old Military Road turn left again. After ½ mile fork left down a narrow track back to the start, instead of walking down the busier road through the village. Distance, about 5 miles.

14 Halmyre, Haugh of Urr   RC

A short road walk. Leave a car at the triangular junction where the road from Milton Loch to Dalbeattie crosses the old Military Road at (826 679). From here walk south for a mile and turn right uphill past the farm of Halmyre. The road then winds downhill with picturesque views of the Urr valley. At the foot of the hill you may turn left and go past the old church with its yew trees, then right along the A710 road, to Haugh of Urr. There turn right at any one of the next three roads, steeply uphill and return to the start in about 1½ miles. The extra section by the church may be omitted by turning right at the foot of the hill. Distance about 4 miles.

SECTION 4
Region between the Castle-Douglas–Gatehouse Road A75 and the coast

1 Glen Isle   RTPRC

Leave car near crossroads at Palnackie. Follow the road to North Glen, through a gap to South Glen and then on to the narrow green neck of land opposite Kippford. A track continues right down to the tip of Glen Isle. A pleasant short walk, and an ideal point frm which to watch the yachts. A return may be made by the track along the edge of the wood on the right rejoining the road near North Glen. (4 miles.)

2 Old Orchardton Tower   RC

This unusual 15th century tower house is thought to be the only tower house built in cylindrical shape - there are lot of square ones. It is under the care of the ministry of the Environment (now the Scottish Office) and is usually open to the public. A pleasant road walk to it starts from palnacknie where a car may be left. Go due south on the secondary road past the school. This winds for a mile up and down to a junction, from which the tower is visible. Turn right and the tower is a few hundred yards on the right. Continue after leaving the tower for another ½ mile to the A711 and turn right again for a mile back to the start at Palnackie. Distance 3½ miles.

3 Almorness RTPRC

Start as in 1, but before reaching South Glen take the rough track to the right—somewhat overgrown. This can, with some difficulty, be followed round the wood past a cottage to emerge on to the road at Almorness House. Turn right there and follow the road back to Palnackie. (6 miles.)

4 Horse Isles Bay and White Port Bay RTPRC

Turn left just after passing through Palnackie down the narrow road to Old Orchardton and Almorness. The car should be left after about 2 miles where a gate indicates the end of the public road. Continue on foot for about 1 mile. Opposite the gate to Almorness House cross a stile and follow the track through the wood to Horse Isles Bay. From there a path leads over the short slope to White Port Bay where there is a fine piece of clean sand and a clear view out to sea. (7 miles.)

NOTE O.S. maps from about 1960 to 1986 had Horse Isles Bay wrongly named as White Horse. The new 1987 editions of the O.S. have corrected the mistake.

5 Heston Island TNTC

A strenuous and tricky excursion but very much worth while. Follow route 3 to White Port Bay. Scramble over the rocks near the water's edge for half a mile to Almorness Point. From here the 'causeway' can be followed on to Heston Island. **Great care** is needed to time this expedition correctly:

(i) It can only be done when a big tide is expected (6 or more metres—see local tables in press).

(ii) Almorness Point should be reached about two hours before low tide or before the causeway is uncovered. The near end of the causeway uncovers last, so that some time may be gained by wading across the first 30-40 fet.

(iii) While some two hours on Heston is possible, the tide must be watched carefully for unexpected changes. The causeway crossing takes about 15 minutes. It is covered in shells and is muddy. (10 miles, plus distance on Heston.)

6   Balcary Heughs   PTC

Car through Auchencairn to Balcary. Cross stile beyond hotel and keep on path to left. This leads along to an old tower, and on round the edge of the rocks to the 'heughs' where the path is on grass above cliffs and care is needed. Return may be made by a track at a wall junction now signposted - Direct to Balcary.

7   Loch Mackie and Rascarrel Bay   RTPRC

Leave car as in 6. Take road uphill at right angles to shore road and go straight on past Airds Cottage along a track. After 1 mile Loch Mackie is reached, nestling at the edge of the trees. Turn left here along a track that leads to the shore. Turn left at the shore and return, as in 6, by the track from the wall junction (4½ miles).

Cliff Path, Balcary Heughs

Screel Hill and Balcary Bay

8 Blackbellie Hill TC

Car to crossroads at (806 560) a mile past Palnackie. Turn up the Gelston Road for ½ mile and leave car opposite a gate into forest on right (802 565). A track leads into the wood. Take the right fork and go round to a pretty cutting through which comes the Mill of Glen Burn. The track circles Blackbellie Hill and rejoins the outgoing route. (3 miles.)

9 Screel Hill and Ben Gairn TNTC*

These attractive hills, although low by Highland standards are rugged and are excellent view points. Access can be got from various points:

(i) On the Palnackie—Auchencairn Road at Chapelyard a road goes up to the right to Gelston (802 545). A few yards up it, on the left, a forestry track leads, after some twists, among the trees, into the Glen of Screel Burn and almost up to the gap to the south-west of Screel. A short scramble leads, on the right, to the top of the Screel. On the left, a slightly longer walk of about 1 mile, over Mid Hill, takes you to Ben Gairn (2½ miles up) but this is now planted and is very rough going.

(ii)   From about (780 570) on the same Gelston Road as above, a diagonal and steep climb may be made directly to the top, over Ingleston Moor (2 miles up).

(iii)   From the road between Gelston and Kirkcudbright a side road to Over Linkins gives access to Arieland Moor and Screel on the left of the Linkins Glen, or on the right, to Ben Gairn (2½ miles up).

(iv)   From the next side road, to Nether Linkins, an approach to Ben Gairn round the side of Ben Tudor may be made (2 miles up).

(v)   From Auchencairn a very rough road leads up to Glenhead and may, with care, be followed to Nether Linkins. From the track a path goes off to the right (763 529) to the gap between Ben Tudor and Ben Gairn. The latter can be reached as in (iv) from the top of this path (1½ miles up).

(vi)   Half a mile before Auchencairn turn right up a narrow road to Bengairn House. Half a mile up this, at a fork, a car may be left. Go up the right fork here, a grassy track, out of the wood on to the moor. There is no path from here on, but the rough, rounded slopes of Ben Gairn are followed to the top, giving good views all the way.

10   Mull of Ross and Meikle Ross   NRPC

Start from the end of the road on the left of Brighouse Bay. A pleasant walk, or scramble, just above the rock round the coast leads to Fauldbog Bay. Here the neck of land may be crossed to the road in Ross Bay. The shore of the bay may however be followed on to the grassy slopes above the rocks of Slack Heugh. This gives a very attractive view of Little Ross Island, and pleasant walking on grass. Turning left at the point and following the shore brings you back to the road at Ross Bay. At the farm there a track leads off on the left over the neck of land back to Brighouse. (Shorter round 2½ miles, longer 5 miles.)

11   Kirkennan Crag   TPNRC

This crag is a well-known landmark just north of the road to Palnackie and about 1 mile before it. It can be reached in several ways, and gives a spectacular view down the Urr to Rough Firth and the Lakeland hills. The best ascent is by the forest track leaving the road opposite the entrance to Kirkennan (826 583). Take the left branches of the track, keeping up and to the left. When the ridge of the forest is reached, the path is difficult to follow; keep left and the path reappears near the crest and is well marked for the last few yards. The rock is exposed and care is needed with children. The return can be made by another track towards Courthill, or back by the same route. About 2 miles.

12 Potterland Hill   TC

Half a mile up the Gelston Road mentioned in No. 8 (i) earlier, a track goes off to the right into the trees. It goes along parallel to the road at first, gradually climbing, and curving to the right. At the most easterly point of a deep little bay a path goes off to the right through the trees and comes out unexpectedly on the crest of the hill above the prominent rock buttress that can be seen from the Auchencairn road. Coming back down the path to the track, this may be followed to the left along, or on to Croach Hill and a rough descent made outside the trees on the west side down to the road opposite Whitehill, about a mile up from the start. Distance about 3 miles.

13 Munches Hill, Buittle, Barlochan   TPRC

A car may be left on the coast road to Palnackie (A711) about ½ mile south of Buittle Bridge. A track goes off on the right, almost opposite the roadend to Breckoneihill. This track swings right along the edge of the trees, then left for ½ mile through the trees to the crest of the hill. At a junction here go sharp right and down to Broomiebrae and then Buittle Church. Turn left here and go down the road, south, for about 2 miles to the coast road again near Barlochan. Turn left for about 2 miles back to the start. Distance, about 5-6 miles.

14 Ben Gairn from Hass   TPNPTC*

The route is mentioned in No. 9 (v). The track at (763 529) leads past the ruined house at Hass. A grassy footpath continues round the hillside and into the dip between Ben Tudor on the left and Tun Hill and curving right is taken to the summit of Ben Gairn (1283 ft.) A return may be made, steeply, due south from the summit towards the house at Hass. Distance about 4 miles.

SECTION 5
Region bounded by the Castle-Douglas Road A75 on the south, the Ken Valley on the west, and the Nith Valley on the north-east

1 Brooklands Hill RTRC

At Crocketford take the back road to Shawhead and turn left in $\frac{1}{4}$ mile, past Meikle Larg. A rough track leads uphill to Larghill and down to the road from Glenkiln. Turn left and down the picturesque Glen of Brooklands to the Corsock Road. Turn left at the junction for Crocketford. (5 miles.)

2 Black Loch RC

About one mile north-east of Kirkpatrick-Durham leave car at junction near Upper Minnydow (790 711). A pleasant narrow road goes up past Black Loch and on to Wellhill. A track continues from there to the Corsock Road and a long circuit could be made (7 miles or return to start (4 miles).

3 Lochenkit Loch PNPC

From just past the roadend to Areeming on the Corsock Road A712 (784 746) a gate on the right gives on to a faint track over the grass on the left of the Areeming Burn. Leave this after about 1 mile and follow the stream on the right to Lochenkit Loch. A pleasant, rough walk round it can be made on the heather. (4-5 miles.)

4 Drumhumphry RPRC

Three walks can be made from the Drumhumphry roadend on the A712 Corsock Road (780 750):

(i)   Take the fork to the right after $\frac{1}{4}$ mile and walk for $1\frac{1}{2}$ miles to Lochenkit Farm. A quarter-mile past it, a track runs off to the left, crosses the Knarie Burn and comes to the road at Auchenhay Farm. Turning left, $2\frac{1}{2}$ miles takes you back to the start. (6 miles.)

(ii)   From the same starting point take the left fork and go on until just past the end of a wood on the left, half a mile before Auchenhay (775 776). A path from here crosses the burn-marshes and comes on to the road from Glaisters. Turn left to get back to the Corsock Road. (5 miles.)

(iii)   A long round may be made by continuing past Auchenhay and following a path north-west along the hillside to Nether Glaisters. From there back by road as in (ii) (8-9 miles).

East Cluden Mill and Water of Cluden
page 19 section 1.

Portling Coast
page 30 section 2.

Castle Point Shore to Skiddaw and Cumbria
page 30 section 2.

Glenkiln King & Queen by Henry Moore
page 54 section 5.

Loch Trool from near the Bruce Stone
page 72 section 7.

Kirkcudbright Heughs to Ross Island
page 89 section 8.

Wanlockhead in Winter
page 97 section 9.

Morton Castle
page 102 section 9.

5   Cairnkinna, 1812 feet   TNT*

This easy hill is distinguished by a very large cairn, and commands a wide view. It lies north-west of Penpont and Tynron and is best approached from Thornhill to either of these village, from whence the road to the Scaur Water is followed north-west. About 1 mile past Woodside at (795 997) a car may be left where a track goes off right uphill steeply, past the ruin of Woodend. There turn left up the rounded ridge and follow this north-west, then north-east to the cairn. Return may be made by east ridge for ½ mile then turning due south back to Woodend and down.

6   Bishop Forest Hill   NC*

By leaving the road at the west end of Glenkiln Reservoir (839 785) a route may be made to the top of Bishop Forest Hill. From there a line due west takes you back to the road at Marglolly Bridge. A short hill walk, but gives good views and is easy going. (3 miles.)

7   Loch Roan

Follow the road from Clarebrand (767 660) running north for 2 miles to a sharp corner at Walbutt where a car may be left. Go through a gate on the right and follow a track round the hill to the pretty Loch Roan with its background of trees. Just after the loch, at (743 696) the track divides into four parts, each giving a possible walk.

(i)   The left branch, round the loch edge, soon stops but a short continuation takes you to the edge of the trees. It is then possible to go along the outside of the wood, keeping to the right, and circle back to the track a little beyond the starting junction. This circuit gives very fine views over Loch Ken and the hills to the west. TNTC. Distance, about 3 miles.

(ii)   The branch second from the left goes on for a mile to join the road from Knockvennie to Parton. About 4 miles there and back. TC.

(iii)   The third branch from the left goes past the old Lochroan farm buildings and shortly goes out of the trees and down north-east, eventually reaching Glenroan Farm and so the road of (ii) above. Turning left here for a mile brings you to the track of (ii) and left again brings you back to the junction. TPRTC. About 5½ miles.

(iv)   The branch farthest to the right gives a short circuit round the wood, coming back to join the track of (iii) and so back to the junction. Distance, 3 miles. TC.

8   Loch Howie and Blackcraig Hill   TNTRC*

Near the summit of the road from Moniaive to New Galloway A702 (690 840) a track goes off to the left and in 1 mile reaches Loch Howie. The east end of this loch is between grassy slopes, the west end between two parts of the forest. The track can be followed round to Laggan and then a beeline made south to the Cairn of Blackcraig Hill at the corner of the forest. Go downhill to the west for about a mile, keeping close to the edge of the forest until the little Loch Brack is reached. Go past its right side on to a forest track that goes left at first, but soon swings round and brings you out to the road at Corriedoo (678 829). Turn right for a mile back to the start. Distance, about 5 miles.

9   Greentop of Margree   TC

This walk starts from the same point on the road A702 from Moniaive to New Galloway as No. 8 above. A gate on the north side of the road gives access to a forestry track. It goes north-west at first and then forks. Take the left fork and pass a cottage on the left, then through a dip between two small round tops; that on the left is Greentop of Margree, and it gives fine views all round. Here the track swings to the east and then south in a big curve, goes round a hillside and past a small loch. In another mile it rejoins the original track at the fork mentioned. Distance, about 6 miles.

10   Lochinvar   RC

From the A702 road from Moniaive to New Galloway at (659 819) a road goes off on the north side. A car may be left here. About 2 miles up this attractive quiet road lies the loch of Lochinvar. This makes a pleasant picnic place and a return may be made by the same route. The road goes on beyond the loch, and there are also numerous paths in the neighbourhood of the loch. Distance out and back, about 4 miles.

11　The Three Glens: Dalwhat, Shinnel and Scaur　RC

These three glens run roughly north-west from Moniaive, Tynron and Penpont respectively. They are quiet and picturesque and give pleasant walks beside the river along the narrow roads. In each a track can be followed past the roadend to the watershed over to the west. Cross-overs can be made if desired through hollows from one glen to the next and a return made down the second glen, giving circular walks.

(i)　DALWHAT WATER. At Moniaive, coming from Dumfries, take the first road to the right after the cross. This road continues for some 6 miles to Cairnhead. A car may be left at Moniaive or at various places farther on and the rest walked. A path goes on for a little beyond Cairnhead.

(ii)　SHINNEL WATER. Tynron may be reached from either the Penpont-Thornhill direction or from Moniaive. Drivers should note that the direct road over the hill from Moniaive is very steep indeed, and they may prefer to go round the few miles extra by Kirkland. The road up the Shinnel Water from Tynron continues for some 6 miles to Shinnelhead. The lower section, as in all these glens, is more wooded, the upper more open. There is no definite path farther. At Bennan, about 2 miles up, a track, then path, goes over the hill to the Scaur Water.

(iii)　SCAUR WATER. One Ordnance Sheet give this name as Scaur, and an adjacent sheet gives Scar. From Penpont go ½ mile south, crossing the river before turning right. The glen goes on for some 12 miles to Polskeoch which is almost on the watershed at about 1200ft. A path continues south-west and joins the road in the valley of the Water of Ken, where a keen cross-over walker could arrange to be picked up. Some 7 miles up from Penpont is the striking rock buttress of Glenwhargen Crag. This gives some scrambling for rock climbers. A walking ascent is easily made from the path on its east side by going up it for about a mile and circling round to the left. This path continues over a dip and descends, in about 5 miles, to Sanquhar. About 10 miles up, at Polgown, another path goes north-east over another dip and also comes down to Sanquhar. See Nos. 12 and 13 below.

12　Scaur Water to Sanquhar by Glenwhargen　PR(X)*

For this crossover walk go by car to Glenwhargen Farm in the

Scaur Valley as in No. 11 (iii). A good path goes up on the west side of the burn, starting just beside the farm. After about a mile it bends right, north-east, for half a mile and then north over the watershed between Shiel Hill and Wether Hill. It continues mainly north for some 2 miles from the watershed, aiming directly for Sanquhar, which can be seen in the distance, and crosses the well-known Deil's Dyke' before crossing the Back Burn. Another 1½ miles brings you to the road near The Kiln. Turn left and follow the road over the Euchan and then the Nith into Sanquhar. Car or bus will then get you back to Dumfries. Distance, Glenwhargen to Sanquhar, about 6 miles.

13 Scaur Water to Sanquhar by Polgown and Cloud Hill   PR(X)*

This cross-over walk starts some 3½ miles farther up the Scaur valley than No. 12, at Polgown. The path goes off on the right of the house, and keeps more or less consistent north-easterly direction all the way. It goes along and up the side of Rough Hill first and after 1½ miles passes just below the top of Cloud Hill (1479 ft), on its right. There is then a slight dip to the watershed, but do not descend to the north here. The path continues north-east, going up again over the shoulder of Welltrees Tappin before going down the left side of the Whing Burn, and joining a track to Ulzieside and then left into Sanquhar. Distance, Polgown to Sanquhar, about 6 miles. This is now part of the Southern Upland Way.

14 Newtonairds and round Steilston Hill   RTPTRC

Newtonairds is on one of the roads from Dumfries to Dunscore, where a bridge across the Cairn joins two of these roads about three miles short of Dunscore. From the north end of the bridge (878 803) go up the farm road and turn up sharp left between the houses. The track goes up steeply at first then swings left and goes on pleasantly between the trees. In about 1½ miles it comes to a small loch. The track continues up to the right, but it is better to try and get on to the path on the left of the loch; the ground is soft and the decision whether to cross just before or just after the loch is best left to visual inspection at the time. The path goes along the edge of the wood, curving right and going through a long narrow belt of trees on the right to a track that leads down to Steilston and the road. Turn right and in 1½ miles return to Newtonairds. Just after the narrow belt of trees a track goes off to the right and returns along and then through the trees to the start at Newtonairds without going down to the road. Distance, about 4-5 miles.

15   Dunscore to Newbridge by Cairn and Cluden   R(X)

Go by bus or car to Dunscore. There go sharp left downhill, the first on the left after the crossroads. The road curves down for some 2 miles to reach the Cairn at Stepford. From here two routes are available:

(i)   Continue on the same, north, side of the river, past the big quarry at Morrington, past Gribton to Newbridge and Dumfries. Distance from Dunscore to Dumfries, about 9 miles. A bus in from Newbridge reduces this to 7 miles.

(ii)   Cross the Cairn by the bridge at Stepford and walk along the road on the south side of the river. After about 2 miles the road swings to the right and forks. At the fork is the bridge 'Routin Bridge' where a fine waterfall is partly under the road at the bridge. Take the left fork here and continue past Irongray to Newbridge as in (i).

16   Shawhead, Glenkiln, Speddoch   R(X)

Shawhead may be reached by car or bus. Go by the road due north downhill through the trees and almost immediately turn left. After about 1½ miles keep straight on up a steep little hill to come to Glenkiln Reservoir. The roadside hereabouts has several statues, placed so as to be seen without leaving the road, by Epstein, Rodin and Moore. Past the reservoir the road goes up a narrow defile to a bridge, Marglolly Bridge. Here keep straight on and soon downhill. A very wide and fine view opens out to the north, as the road winds down to Speddoch. Distance, Shawhead to Speddoch, about 6½ miles. If a car is not available to pick you up here, it is another 2½ miles into Dunscore and a bus.

Glenkiln Statues No. 16A See sketch map.

The positions of the statues are shown on the sketch map. Three are on roadsides, the other four are on the hillsides nearby and may be approached on foot. The statues are:-

1	JB	John the Baptist	by Rodin
2	SF	Standing figure	by Moore
3	KG	King and Queen	by Moore
4	DK	Glenkiln Cross	by Moore
5	2F	Two figures	by Moore
6	M	The Maiden	by Epstein
7	ES	Elephant Stone	by Thurber

Note that No. 7 is quite different from the others. It is on a large granite stone on the hillside with only outlines faintly visible. It was done by the U.S. humorous writer Thurber, for what reason is not known.

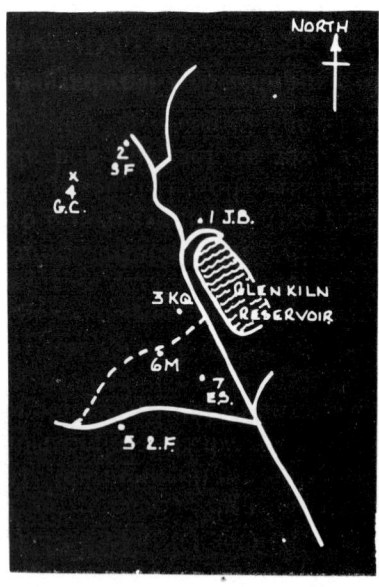

17 Glenkiln, Marglolly Bridge, Nether Craigenputtock, Lettrick RTP(X)

The start of this walk may be at Shawhead as in No. 16 above, or it may be shortened by taking the car to the reservoir at Glenkiln and starting from there. Walk up the road to Marglolly Bridge and turn left along the moor road. This road goes past the farms of Muil and Slongaber, after which it becomes a rough moorland track. After a mile, with fine open views and exposed to all the winds, it reaches the ruins of Darngarroch. From there it goes slightly left to the road in Glenesslin at a clump of trees beside Nether Craigenputtock. Recent plantings may require some diversion in this last section near the house known in the new O.S. maps as Lettrick. Distance from Glenkiln, about 6 miles. If a car cannot be arranged to meet the walker here, he can turn right for about 5 miles to Dunscore, or turn left for about 5½ mile to Corsock. There is a more frequent bus service from Dunscore that from Corsock.

18 Glenesslin, Loch Urr, Moniaive R(X)

This walk starts in Glenesslin about a mile east of the finish of NO. 17 at the fork at (800 841). If the start is made from Dunscore the distance is increased by some 4 miles. Go along the right branch, uphill in a westerly direction, on a pleasant moor road for about a mile to the top, then downhill towards Loch Urr in the distance. At the junction after the loch keep right and in another mile join the A702 road from Moniaive to New Galloway. Turn right again for some 3 miles into Moniaive. Distance from start suggested to Moniaive, 7½ miles.

19 Fell Hill PNPC*

Fell Hill lies some 2 miles west of Loch Urr and is easily reached from the road on its west side. From Moniaive follow the A702 road of No. 18 for some 3 miles and turn left. At the fork before Loch Urr go right for a mile to a little bridge, where a car may be left. A path goes along the east side of the burn towards the old cottage of Fell, from which it is a short scramble to the top of Fell Hill (1368 ft). A circuit may be made on the moor to return to the start or the path followed down again. There is a good view from the top, over the surrounding moors. Distance up and down, 4 miles.

20 Lochenkit Loch and Milharay   RPNPRC*

From Crocketford on the A75 go for about 1½ miles along the A712 in the direction of Corsock, to the crossroads at (806 727) where a car may be left. Walk up the road on the right through a well-wooded glen for a mile. At the end of the plantation, the rough tops of Milharay are seen on the left. A walk of about a mile over rought heathery ground takes you to the cairn (972 ft), from which a fine view is obtained. Lochenkit Loch is seen below, to the north, and is easily reached across the moor. A path leads from the loch, at its west end and on its north side, back to the Corsock road some two miles from the starting point. Distance, about 6 miles. (See No. 3 above.)

21 Lochenkit Loch and The Bennan   PNRC*

Go to the crossroads mentioned in No. 20 and take a car for 1½ miles up the narrow road to where a track comes in from the right, at a bridge (816 745). From here a path goes off on the left, over the moor, passing near the Martyrs' Tomb and Monument. The path curves to the right and the loch is seen below to the left. After visiting the loch (if desired; the path does not go down to it), a beeline can be made across the moor to the north-east for about 1½ miles towards the big cairn on the top of The Bennan (1306 ft). This cairn is Turner's Monument and is visible from many places in the district; an extensive view is obtained from it. From the cairn descend direct to the road in a south-east direction for about a mile, to a point near Glen Farm. Turn right along the road for about 1½ miles back to the car. Distance, about 5 miles.

22 Memorial Monuments Walks See colour photographs

Three of the monuments shown in the photographs are strikingly situated on the hilltops and can be seen for many miles away. The fourth monument, to Covenanting Martyrs, is decently hidden in a hollow. All are reached by attractive walks, the three hilltop ones also giving fine views.

1 Turner's Monument p.56 no. 21. Turner was a shepherd who wished to be buried on his local hill and his friends erected the monument to him.

2   The Martyrs' Monument - p.56 no. 21, is in a hollow about a mile south of Turner's and the grave of the martyrs is close by in a little walled enclosure. The monument is surmounted by a hand pointing heavenward.

3   Neilson's Monument. Neilson was the inventor of the blast furnace used for steel making. It is on the top of the small hill Back Fell (683 607) about three miles west of Castle Douglas. It can be seen on the skyline from the A75 as Ringford is approached. Turn right at Ringford up the A762 towards Laurieston. About a mile up, near Waterside, a grassy track goes off on the right. A car may usually be left about here. The track goes along the east side of the hill. After about half a mile incline left up the hillside towards the monument - there is no proper path. Other approaches are even steeper. From the top there is a good view all round and down to Bargatton Loch. Return by the same route. Distance 2 miles.

4.   The Huntsman's Monument. PNPC. The Hunstman was Joe Graham of the Annandale and Eskdale Hunt and the monument was erected by his friends. It is unusual in having, as well as the name plate, a large oval copper scene depicting the Hunt. It may be seen from the road junction at Lochmaben at the War Memorial Park as a speck on the far hillside to the right of the Castle Loch. The approach is, however, better made from the west, from the A75 road. Turn off about $1\frac{1}{2}$ miles east of Collin, at Breconrae and follow the secondary road uphill and down, with fine views, for about $2\frac{1}{2}$ miles to (092745) where a narrow road goes off left to Kirkhill Farm. The monument should now be seen on the skyline beyond the farm and advice sought. A series of gates leads up to the ridge and the monument and there is usually no difficulty in obtaining permission to visit it. Return by the same route. Distance about 2 miles.

23   Mochrum Fell (1039 ft)   RNRC*

Car from Corsock to the corner at Lower Ardmannoch (742 731). A narrow side road to the north leads past Ardmannoch to Mochrum House at the foot of the Fell. A track to the right leads on to the east slopes. Turn west up the slopes to the top. A surprisingly good viewpoint and a pleasant short walk. (5 miles out and back from Lower Ardmannoch.) Another track goes west from Mochrum and circles the hill.

24   Black Loch Walks   RPRPRC

(i)   Turn off from the A75 road 2 miles after Crocketford by a narrow straight road and in about a mile turn left. After ½ mile take the right fork uphill, passing the Black Loch after a mile, and continuing for another ½ mile to the roadend from Bardarroch Farm. With some care a car can be left about here. Walk north for about a mile, passing Wellhill and turn left (west) along a track at (780 734). This leads past a small pond to Arkland and the road down the Urr valley in about a mile from Wellhill. Turn left down the road for about 1½ miles. Turn left again opposite the Glenlair roadend (764 721) and go up another track. This goes uphill at the edge of a wood of fine beeches for ½ mile. The path forks at (769 716); take the left fork and continue north-east for about a mile back to Bardarroch. Distance about 5 miles.

(ii)   Go as in (i) to the fork at (769 716) and take the right fork. This goes south-east and joins the track to Pipercroft, which you pass on the left. Continue for another ½ mile until just past the roadend on the right to Barmoffity. At a corner at (783 709) a path goes off sharply to the left at a gate, and leads over a pleasant hilltop down to the corner of the Black Loch at the road (785 719), ½ mile south of the car at Bardarroch. Distance, about 5½ miles.

25   Shawhead, Old Clouden   RC

From Dumfries go out the back road through Terregles towards Shawhead. About 5 miles out, as (894 762) there is a steep little dip where the road crosses Barnshalloch Bridge. Turning right here it is possible, with some care, to leave a car nearby. Walk along the side road past Knockshinnoch and Old Clouden and turning west cross the bridge over the Old Water of Cluden. Turn left here for a mile to Shawhead crossroads, then left again for 1½ miles back to the start. Distance, about 3½ miles.

26 Shawhead, Old Clouden, Larbreck, Midrig RTRC

On the road from Shawhead to Routin Bridge a car may be left near the Rosebank Bridge over the Old Water of Cluden. Do not cross the bridge but walk along the track on the east side of the burn to Old Clouden. From there continue in a north-east direction by the track that runs along the hillside above the burn to Larbreck in about a mile. Just before Larbreck turn left downhill, then left again and cross the burn to Midrig. Turn left again and return in about 2 miles to the start. Distance, 4-5 miles.

27 Crochmore, Larbreck, Old Clouden RTC

On the back road to Shawhead, as in No. 25, leave a car near the side road near Bonerick (904 766). Walk along this side road past Meikle Barncleugh, Crochmore, and then up and over a surprisingly steep little hill and down to Larbreck. Continue from there as in No. 26. At the bridge opposite Old Clouden (877 771) turn left and at Barnshalloch Bridge left again to return to the start. Distance, about 5 miles. For a slightly longer round, instead of turning left to Old Clouden, continue for another mile into Shawhead before turning left. This increases the distance by a little over a mile.

28 Irongray, Horsebog Loch, Routin Bridge PNTRC

A car may be left near the bridge or the church at Irongray (917 796). A short distance west, just after a small burn, a path goes steeply uphill beside the burn and then curves to the right, continuing uphill. It leads to a wide valley, usually rather marshy in the middle, with the small pond rejoicing in the name of Horsebog Loch. The going hereabouts is usually better on the north, right, side, a bit up from the lowest levels. Shortly after passing the 'loch', a track will be reached passing Lag and joining the track of No. 26 from Larbreck. Follow this over the river to Midrig and turn right. After a mile the bridge and waterfall at Routin Bridge is reached. Here turn right for 2 miles to the starting point. Distance, about 5½ miles.

29 Shawhead, Peartree Hill, Glen Burn, Shawhead RPRC

From Shawhead go along the back road towards Crocketford for 1½ miles. Turn right at Peartree Cottage (853 754) up a grassy track which goes past a ruined cottage soon after which the track forks.

(i)   The right fork goes on for a little then curves to the right and to the road to the Glenkiln reservoir. Turn right at the road for a mile and a half back to Shawhead. Distance, about 4½ miles.

(ii)   The left fork goes along an old track, aiming for a gap between two patches of trees near the crest of the hill, for about a mile. Here the track, if visible, should be left and a beeline made by a faint path downhill towards the farm of Glen which is immediately opposite. At Glen turn right down the road and at the bridge at the bottom turn right again as in (i) for Shawhead. Distance, 6-7 miles.
Or

(iii)   Instead of turning downhill towards Glen Farm, continue diagonally left down a re-made track, reaching the road about a mile south-west of Glen. Turn right as before, to return to Shawhead. Distance, 8-9 miles.

30   Garcrogo Forest   TRC or TNRC

On the A712 road from Crocketford to New Galloway, some 2 miles after Corsock, is the start of Garcrogo Forest. A turning to the right here, with room to leave a car, indicates the start of the walk. After about a mile fork left for half a mile where (717 794) you meet a track leading down left to Garcrogo Farm and back to the road about a mile and a half from the start. Distance, round about 4 miles. For a slightly longer and rougher walk, at the point (717 794) mentioned above follow a path north, which disappears after a bit. Continue, in a north-west direction, to the edge of the wood about ½ mile to the west of Blackcraig Farm and turn left for a mile back to the A712. In spite of the sign here it is unlikely that you will be able to obtain either Bread or Beer! About 2½ miles along the road brings you back to the starting point. Distance, about 6 miles.

31   Ardmannoch, Poundland, Mochrum   RTRC

This is an attractive road with a forest track and two lochans. Its starting point is at the junction at (738 735) near Ardmannoch. This point may be reached either from Corsock on A712 or from the south by B794. From the junction, walk west for about 1 mile to the second forest track that goes off on the right (725 726). This winds on for about a mile and comes out above two small Pattieshorn lochans, turning east and then north for another mile towards Mochrum. At the next junction turn east towards Mochrum, and at it turn right again (south) back to Ardmannoch. Distance, 4 ½ miles.

32 Lochenkit Farm and Drumhumphry Burn   PRC

Leave the Corsock road at the same point as in No. 3, p. 48. After crossing the burn that comes from Lochenkit Loch continue northeast for another mile, past the east side of a small wood, by a rather faint path. Pass on the west (left) side of a small rounded hill and join at (800 767) another path from the east (right). Turn left along this other path towards Lochenkit Farm in its small clump of trees some half a mile west. From the farm a road leads pleasantly down the burnside to the Corsock road in 1½ miles, a little west of the starting point. Distance about 5 miles.

33 Corsock to Ardmannoch   RTPRC

At Corsock on A712 a side road goes off to the south just opposite the school. Follow this for about a mile, turning west, to a triple junction at (748 761). The tarred road goes straight on to Black Arvie Farm, but you take the left hand track along the edge of the trees. After a quarter of a mile you see the little Arvie Loch and the track curves left on to the open hill. It then becomes a path and curves right to the edge of a narrow wood and continues for another mile to the tarred road at (737 741) near Ardmannoch. Turn left for a mile to the junction at Lower Ardmannoch. Turn left again here and follow the winding pleasant road for some 3 miles back to Corsock, just below the church. Distance about 6-7 miles.

34 Nether Craigenputtock and Darngarroch   TPNPTC*

This is a rough walk right up on the open moors. Follow the secondary road from Dunscore up Glen Esslin to Nether Craigenputtock at (789 831) where there is a farm on the right and a private house, Lettrick, on the left. A gate gives access here to the old track over the moors south to, eventually, Marglolly Bridge (see No. 6, p.49). This track may be followed (with some difficulty — it is rough) to the ruined farm at Darngarroch. Here turn left and go norht-east for about a mile to the cairn on Darngarroch Hill (1224 ft). From this point go downhill west to rejoin the outward track. Distance about 4 miles. This walk is almost the reverse of Section 5, 17, p. 54.

35 Loch Howie and Loch Skae T

Follow the road from Moniaive to New Galloway, A702 to its summit at (690 840), where a car may be left. (See No. 8, p.50). A track on the left (south) side leads after about a mile to Loch Howie. Follow this track round to the ruins of Laggan. From here a track continues uphill on the left in an easterly direction for about a mile, curving gradually south and arriving at the picturesque little Loch Skae. Return by the same route. Distance to Loch Skae, about 2 miles.

36 Loch Brack from Troquhain NC*

Follow the Corsock — New Galloway road A712 to just before Troquhain (683 796) where a car may be left in a convenient quarry. From here go directly up on to the moor on the right, past a large sheep pen. Troquhain Loch is seen below on the left. A pleasant grassy walk then takes you in a northerly direction uphill to a dip to the left of a stony skyline ridge. From this dip another, rough, half mile takes you down to Loch Brack nestling in the trees. The return may be made by the same route, or by keeping along the edge of the forest, south-west, the cairn on the top of Barscobe Hill may easily be reached and a course taken back across the moor to the starting point. Distance about 4-5 miles.

37 Lochs Roan, Smaddy and Lurkie TPRTC

See No. 7 (ii) p.49. Just after starting along the second branch leading to the Parton road a grassy track goes off left and through a gate. This takes you immediately on to the open hillside, with good views to the west and north. The track winds down towards the little round Loch Smaddy passing it on its north-east side and into a wood with a ruined cottage. A damp and faint path continues through a clearing in the wood, curving left and comes down towards Barwhillanty Farm on the road down to Parton. Here turn right uphill past Loch Lurkie. After half a mile a gate on the right leads to a metalled track south that takes you back to Loch Roan. Distance about 5 miles from the start at Walbutt.

38 Barlay, Craig and Shaw Fell TPTC or TPNTC*

Leave the Corsock—New Galloway road A712 at a junction at (700 793) signposted to Barlay and Craig. This pleasant little road winds for some 3-4 miles to a sharp corner near Craig. A car may be left about here (679 757). A track goes off south and before turning up to the farm of Upper Dullarg a path continues south along the hillside towards Nether Dullarg. The path can be followed to Nether Dullarg, then turning left a further path to Little Merkland in half a mile and on to Glenswinton. From here another path goes off north-west and winds over the moor back to the roadend near Craig. Instead of following this sequence of paths, the path to Nether Dullarg may pleasantly be left after a mile and the knobbly hillside followed to the top of Shaw Fell (737 ft). From it the return path is easily reached downhill. Distance about 5-6 miles, a little less on the hill.

39   Halfmark and moorpath   TPN

A short pleasant walk on a quiet road and an open moor, with good views and possible variations.

From Corsock take the road north to Moniaive. After 2 miles at a fork keep left and after another mile fork left again. After a further mile a narrow rough track goes off on the right to Halfmark. A car may be left here beside a row of beech trees. Walk up the track for a mile past Halfmark and on to the hillside. A path continues more or less straight on uphill towards the obvious dip in the skyline ahead.

This dip, at a fence, is a good picnic spot. Immediately ahead and below is a view of the little Loch Skae (No. 35). It would be possible to turn right along the fence and reach Fell Hill (No. 19) and return from there across the moor to the car, but rough. Distance to dip and back about 4 miles.

40   Knocksting Loch   TC

This is a quiet upland loch, with grassy slopes and open views on one side and trees on the other. Take the A702 road from Moniaive to Dalry for about 3 miles just past Castlefairn to where a track goes off on the right at a group of cottages, at (732 869). A car may usually be left here. Follow this track keeping right at the first fork and go up along the burn for about a mile. Here, at another fork, take the left fork and cross the burn. Go uphill for about another mile when a further short spur to the right brings you to the loch. There are pleasant grassy slopes round part of the loch, but a return by the same route is probably best. Distance about 4-5 miles there and back.

41 New Loch Walk RTC

A very attractive and secretive little loch. Recently formed in the forest it has as yet no name on the new O.S. 1:50,000 map. Take the B729 road from Moniaive to Carsphairn for some 5 miles to a fork at (690910) near the summit. A car may be left here at a lay-by. Go through the gate on the left fork. After about a mile at a small plantation, turn left and continue for about another mile, past a gate marked 'Private Road' (permissible for walkers). A little farther on is a 4-way junction. Turn left, skirting another gate. The track continues between the trees. After half a mile turn right on the track and continue downhill. A glimpse of the loch is seen through a gap. Continue on the track uphill for a litte, then turn right and go downhill to the little loch and its dam. At the end of the track, at the dam is a watcher's hut. Return by the same route. Distance about 3 miles each way, total about 6 miles. Locally known as Mackay's Loch.

SECTION 6
The Rhinns of Kells, Carsphairn to New Cumnock

The character of the Galloway hills is quite different from that of the Lowther and Moffatdale groups. They are more of the Highland type—more rocky, more heathery, with great wide uninhabited basins full of bog. Their colours are different from the smooth green slopes of the Dumfriesshire hills. But it is impossible to compare the aesthetic values of these different qualities. The writer has seen wonderful colours and cloud formations in both groups. The Galloway group excels in colour and in all those details that make up wilderness; but the Moffatdale group, especially around Blackhope Glen—and to some extent the Durisdeer hills—excel in the beauty of form and line, of steep unbroken curves, and depths of narrow glen. The best thing to say is that each group is attractive in its own way.

1 Craigshinnie Glen RC

A pleasant road walk in a quiet and picturesque glen. From New Galloway take the Ayr road A762 to Glenlee but go straight on for a $\frac{1}{4}$ mile after the Ayr road turns right and crosses the river. A narrow road goes off left steeply uphill. A car may be left about here. Follow the narrow road uphill, alongside the burn and trees. After about $2\frac{1}{2}$ miles Clatteringshaws can be seen ahead. The road curves left and joins the A712 (Queensway) road. A car could come round from the start to pick up walkers here, or a return may be made by the same route back to the start. Distance there and back about 6 miles.

2 Meikle Millyea (2448 ft) and Loch Dungeon NC*

Continue as in 1 past Glenlee, without crossing the river. A charming winding road goes up for some 4-5 miles to Clenries, but a car may well be left where the surface deteriorates at Drumbuie (567 822). At a burn half a mile farther on, leave the road for the moor and make for the Rig of Clenrie and then for the east ridge leading to Meikle Millyea. Notice that from the Rig to the summit is almost a semicircle, and in poor visibility care with change of direction is necessary. A return may be made by the same route. (7 miles.)

An alternative route is to keep to the lower ground between the Rig of Clenrie and the forest on the right, and head for the gap between the forest and the steep slopes of Meikle Millyea; at the corner of the forest keep along the fence and Loch Dungeon appears ahead and below. The ground here is very rough. A wide gap between the rocks gives a steep but easy scramble to the ridge. A steeper climb can be got by following one of the gullies of the two burns coming into the south-west corner of Loch Dungeon. These lead to the col between Meikle Millyea and Milldown but should only be attempted by the experienced as some rock scrambling may be needed.

3 Forrest Lodge and Corserine (2669 ft) TPNTC*

Follow the Ayr road from Dalry to Polharrow Bridge and turn off to the left. A good road goes for 4-5 miles to near Forrest Lodge where a car may be left. Follow the track from the bridge up the burn to Fore Bush. From there a forestry track now curves to the right round the hillside, which is now planted with trees. The climber should bear left from the end of this track up on to the slopes of North Gairy Top and so to Corserine in about 4½ miles from Forrest Lodge. The former path, which is still shown on some maps, kept to the lower slopes, making for the lowest point of the ridge about 1½ miles south of Corserine from where it continues downhill to Back Hill of Bush cottage. A return to Forrest Lodge can be made from Corserine by coming about ½ mile east and then following the north-east ridge over Polmaddy Gairy and Craigrine. At any suitable point here make a beeline over the moor for Loch Harrow, Fore Bush and so Forrest Lodge. The going on the lower ground here is very rough. (9 miles).

4 Corserine (2669 ft), Carlin's Cairn (2600 ft), and Meaul (2281 ft) TPNTC*

Follow No. 3 to the top of Corserine. Then walk north along the ridge over the top of Carlin's Cairn and on to the next top of Meaul. This is the narrowest and finest part of the ridge and gives fine views in all directions. From the top of Meaul turn east over Cairnsgarroch and down to one of the forest tracks below. From Castlemaddy a track can be taken across the river and over the hill by a cairn, back to Forrest Lodge. This is a long expedition of some 14-15 miles.

5 Coran of Portmark (2042 ft)   TNTC*

About a mile north of Carsphairn turn up the road on the left to Garryhorn. A car may be left there or thereabouts. Follow the track up to the old lead mines. A path continues west up the slopes leading to the Coran of Portmark. The ridge here may be followed south over the small tops of Bow and a return made down the ridge of Cairnsgarroch to the lead mines. (7-8 miles.)

The path from the lead mines to the north-west can be followed through a shallow dip and down to the shores of Loch Doon. A passage could then be made round the south end of Loch Doon to the roadend on the west side if suitable transport were arranged. (5-6 miles.)

6 The Rhinns of Kells   TNT(X)*

For the ambitious the traverse of the Rhinns in one day is a fine expedition. A car takes you to the start below Clenries (as in No.2) and the ridge is reached at Meikle Millyea. The ridge is then followed north to the Coran of Portmark and a descent made to the lead mines and Garryhorn where transport may wait. The distance to walk is some 13-14 miles: and there is a good deal of up and down.

7 Cairnsmore of Carsphairn (2514 ft)   PNPC*

(i) From Knockgray. A car may be left near the farm of Knockgray, about 1 mile east of Carsphairn, and a track followed up the burnside from there. Go almost due north across the moor and on to the west ridge of the hill. Follow the wide ridge to the top, from where a very extensive view is got on a clear day. Leave the top in a south-east direction and go over the rounded top of Beninner before turning south-west for Knockgray across the moor. (about 7 miles.)

(ii) Alternative route.
> 'There's Cairnsmore of Fleet,
> And Cairnsmore of Dee,
> And Cairnsmore of Carsphairn:
> The biggest of the three.'

So says the Galloway rhyme. Another way to get to this rather remote hill is via Moniaive, from which you follow the moorland road towards Carsphairn, but branch right immediately after crossing the Water of Ken. Go along this for 2 miles to the cottage of

Craigengillan. A track goes up left towards the house at Moorbrock and a car may be left about there. From here a path goes south-west. After about ½ mile leave the path and turn west making for the steep slopes of Beninner Gairy. Once on its ridge turn right (north) for the top (2329 ft). A small dip and then a rise brings the walker in another mile to the top of Cairnsmore (2614 ft). On the return, a descent may be made from the dip, north-eastwards down to the Poldores Burn and the burn followed back to Moorbrock. Distance about 6 miles.

8   Alwhat, Alhang, Windy Standard   NC*

A car may be taken as in No. 7, up the Water of Ken Road, but going some 5 miles up from the roadend to the bridge near Dalquhairn. From here a pleasant hill circuit may be made. From the bridge go due north up the steep slope of Ewe Hill and then dip down north-west and up to Alwhat (2064 ft). From the top a fine view down the length of the Afton Reservoir is obtained. Turning almost due south another dip and rise brings the walker in a mile to Alhang (2100 ft). From here the route turns north-west, dips for about a mile and 500 ft before rising again steeply to Windy Standard. In poor visability some care is needed here; at the lowest point do not follow the boundary fence north-west—turn due west, crossing two small burns and make straight for the, rather flat, top. The cairn is at the north end (2290ft). The return is best made from the cairn south-east for about ½ mile, until near the edge of the steeper slopes on the left, then south for about ½ mile until a path running east is met (624 002). Turning left along this path leads you back to Dalquhairn. It should be obvious that if there is mist on the hills this is not a suitable route for inexperienced navigators. Distance about 8 miles.

9   Lamloch and Loch Doon   TNC*

Go by car to Carsphairn on the A713 road and about 2½ miles north of it turn down to the left to Lamloch. A car may be left near here. A forestry track goes on from here in a generally north-westerly direction to a dip between two small hills and then drops down to the side of Loch Doon. A return may be made by the same route, but a different route adds interest. Go up on to the small hill, Craigencolon, just south of the outward track, and turn south along the ridge leading to Black Craig (1731 ft). This ridge walk and top gives a very fine view of the Merrick hills and the Dungeon of Buchan beyond the south end of Loch Doon. From the top of Black Craig a direct line downhill towards Lamloch is made; it is steep and rough and there is no path. Distances: (i) out and back, about 4 miles; (ii) over Black Craig, about 5 miles.

10 Polmaddy Burn and Polmaddy Forest   TC

On the A713 road from Dalry to Carsphairn, about half-way, a forestry track goes off on the left at Polmaddie (598 880). A car may be left about here. This attractive road winds up through the trees for some 6 miles, on the north side of the Polmaddy Burn. The track goes into the corrie at the foot of the steep upper slopes of the Rhinns of Kells between Carlin's Cairn on the left and Meaul on the right; or it could be used as a route off the hill down to Polmaddie.

11 Cruffel, 1826 ft, Corse Hill, 1909 ft   NC*

These two hills lie south-west of Sanquhar, south of the Euchan Water. A car may be left near Glenglass, some 5 miles up the Euchan Water. Cross the river by the bridge at Glenglass and so on to the rounded north-east ridge of Cruffel. From the rounded top there is a small drop to the surprisingly large Polvaird Loch, situated at some 1750 ft. Going past the loch on the east side a rough walk of about a mile, in a direction a little west of south, takes you to the Ordnance pillar visible on Corse Hill. There are good views all round from here; Glenwhargen Crags are well seen to the east. A return may be made by the long Black Shoulder to the west of the outward route. This brings you back to the Euchan Water at the ruin of Euchan Head and so down the burn-side for some 2 miles back to Glenglass. The going here is very rough. Distance, 6-7 miles.

Or go up the Scaur Water as in Section 5, No. 13, p.52 to Polgown and curve uphill until the fence is reached running west to a sharp corner. Turn north on a ridge that goes past Polvaird Loch and on with a slight rise to Cruffel. If a cross-over is arranged this makes a good expedition from Euchan to Scaur or in reverse. NC(X)*

12 St. John's Town of Dalry, New Bridge Walks PR

The construction of a footbridge over the Water of Ken in connection with the Southern Upland Way gives an attractive short walk from Dalry. Leave Dalry by the path signposted for the Southern Upland Way and go across the bridge. Follow the path until it joins the A762 Ayr road. Turn right and follow the road round by Milton Park back to Dalry. Distance about 1½ miles.

SECTION 7
Newton Stewart to Dalmellington west of Rhinns of Kells

This is the wildest and most rugged part of Galloway. On the hills, boots and protective clothing are advisable; map and compass and the knowledge to use them are essential. Poor weather can come up quickly from the west and some of the ground is very boggy.

` Many of the best walks are 'cross-overs' for which transport at the other end must be arranged.

1 Clatteringshaws to Loch Doon TNT(X)

Turn off the A712, New Galloway—Newton Stewart Road at (567 771) a mile before Clatteringshaws. This road can be followed for 2 miles to a turning on the left with a locked gate. From here a forestry road can be walked up the Dee, on to Back Hill of Bush and up to the watershed past the March Burn. From here keep a little up the slopes on the east, away from the softest going until the track round the south end of Loch Doon is reached. A car can wait at the Carrick Lane on the west side at (476 942). Distance to walk, about 13-14 miles.

2 Old Edinburgh Road to Murray's Monument TP(X)

Turn off from A712 to the right just after the dam at Caltteringshaws (545 749) and go round half a mile to the bay at Pulran Burn. From here a forestry track has been made along the dip to the west. After about a mile Lilie's Loch is reached. The path goes along the south side and down to the Poultrybuie Burn. Cross this and continue along the south side of Black Loch and down the steep but picturesque path beside the falls on the Grey Mare's Tail Burn to the main road. Another forestry road now goes from Craigdews round by Black Loch almost back to the main road at Murray's Monument. (About 4 miles.)

3 Loch of the Lowes P(X)

From Murray's Monument take the path up the Grey Mare's Tail Burn. Where it levels out, turn left and cross the burn into the trees.

This track is the continuation of the Old Edinburgh Road of No. 2 and can be followed for some 2 miles west to the little Loch of the Lowes. A farther two miles brings you to a side road where, turning left, half a mile brings you back to A712 at (442 678). About 5 miles.

4   Craignell and Darnaw   TNTC*

Follow the route of No. 2 to Lilie's Loch. From there cut up to the right, up steep slopes, on to the ridge of Craignell. From there a pleasant walk along the top, past several small lochans brings you to Low Craignell. Turn left here, or earlier, and go down the north-east ridge of Darnaw to the Half Way Stone on the road and turn right back to the start. About 6 miles. On Darnaw is a memorial to a crashed plane.

5   Craigdews to Craigencallie   TN(X)

At Craigdews on A712 (505 726) a forestry track leads up the Poultrybuie Burn and round to Black Loch. Before the loch, a branch sweeps uphill in a great curve and goes round Poultrybuie Hill, over the watershed, past Munwhul and down by the Fore Burn to join the road in No. 2 near Craigencallie. This forest track is occasionally open for cars. Distance, Craigdews to Craigencallie, about 4 miles.

6   Millfore (2152 ft)   TNTC*

Leave the A712 at Craigdews as in No. 5 and go up to the cairn on Poultrybuie Hill. From here follow the long south-east ridge of Millfore to the cairn on the top. The main ridge runs south-west from the highest point, with the several other cairns on it, and a small lochan. If the ridge is followed to here, a return may be made south-east back to the Grey Mare's Tail Burn, but the flatter, lower ground is usually very wet going. The path by the Black Loch may be followed back to Craigdews. (6-7 miles.) (See also No. 8.)

7   Craigencallie to Loch Trool   TNT(X)

This is another very fine cross-over route, but rough going in places. As in No. 2 turn off A712 and follow the side road to a turning place on the road just before the trees at Craigencallie. A car may be left about here. Follow the forestry track past Craigencallie and on to the moor. The track contours the hillside, but when Loch Dee is sighted the ground is rough. The sandy shores of Loch Dee may be visited. The forestry track now continues past the renovated White Laggan Bothy and crosses the burn by a bridge. The track on the other side is some hundred feet up the hillside. It crosses the watershed and goes down the right—north—side of the Glenhead Burn, some height above the burn until near Glenhead. From Glenhead the road leads past Buchan and the Bruce Stone to the car park where transport will be welcomed. (6-7 miles, Craigencallie to Bruce Stone.) Part of the Southern Upland Way may also be followed from near the watershed to Caldons on Loch Trool.

8 Millfore (2152 ft) from Craigencallie   NC*

Leave car near Craigencallie as in No. 7. Go up the slopes in a south-west direction to the col and follow the long ridge south to the cairn on Millfore. A descent may be made eastwards, in the direction of Munwhul, and then the forestry road of No. 6 followed back to Craigencallie.In leaving the cairn of Millfore, care must be taken not to go north, where steep rocks are encountered, before turning east. (5 miles.)

9 Cairngarroch (1829 ft)   NC*

The rocky hill behind Craigencallie gives a fine view of the hills round the 'Dungeon'. From Craigencallie, as in No. 8, go up to the col and turn right, reaching the top in half a mile. A descent may be made due north, but care must be taken not to turn east above the steep rocks. (4 miles.)

10 Curlywee (2212 ft)   *

This is the most mountainous looking of the Galloway hills, and his comparatively inaccessible. But it is well worth a visit, and can be reached from all sides:

(i) From CALDONS on Loch Trool follow the track up the Caldon Burn on to Cambrick Hill on the left and Lamachan (2350 ft). Follow the narrow ridge due east down to the Nick of Curlywee and then up steeply to the summit. Return by the same route. (9-10 miles.) (PNPC)

(ii)   From LOCH TROOL (TPNC) walk from the car park up the road to Glenhead, the follow the path to Loch Dee (as in No. 7). Just before Loch Dee turn south up the slopes of Curlywee to the top. The last part is fairly steep. A return may be made by the same route (9-10 miles) or by the route over Lamachan as in (i) above.

(iii)   From CRAIGENCALLIE (TNTC) follow the forestry track as in No. 7 but go up the White Laggan Burn for a little before crossing to the east slopes of Curlywee and ascending them to the top. Returning by the same route, the distance is about 10 miles.

(iv)   From CRAIGENCALLIE (NC) follow the route as in No. 8 to the col south of Cairngarroch and descend to the White Laggan. Cross this and go up to Curlywee as in (iii) above. This shortens the distance to walk at the expense of extra height to climb and lose again. (About 6-7 miles.)

(v)   From MINNIGAFF (TPNPTC). The road up the Penkiln Burn should be taken as far as possible, to Drigmorn and then go up the east side of the burn. The old pony track from here over the col to the east of Bennan Hill is now partly lost in the forest, and the going is very rough. The pony track continues towards Loch Dee and the rebuilt bothy of White Laggan. Leave the track at its highest point, about (457 761), and go up the slopes on the left to Curlywe. A return may be made over Lamachan and then, turning south over Larg Hill. From Larg Hill a descent to the east take you to a forest track and back to the road at Garlick, near Auchinleck. Round distance, from Auchinleck about 10-11 miles.

11   Lamachan (2350 ft) and Larg Hill (2216 ft)   PNPC*

Proceed as in No. 10 by the first route to Curlywee as far as the top of Lamachan. Turn south along the ridge, then south-west and up the ridge to Larg Hill. There is a further small top on Larg Hill another half mile south-west. The return to Caldons is best made by retracing one's steps to the col between Larg Hill and Lamachan and going down the broad north-west slopes to Craignaw before striking down to the Caldon Burn on the right. (7-8 miles.)

12   Craigencallie, Loch Dee, Craiglee (1743 ft)   PNPC*

Proceed as in No. 7 from Craigencallie for about 1½ miles until just before the burn running from Cairngarroch to the east end of

Loch Dee. Make for the east end of the loch, where there is now a footbridge. Make straight for the cairn on Craiglee, about a mile to the north-west. The cairn makes a pleasant lunch spot, with fine views down to Loch Trool and the surrounding hills. (6 miles).

13   Snibe Hill, Craignaw (2115 ft) and the Silver Flow   NC*

Permission may sometimes be obtained to take a car up the forestry road described in No. 1 towards Back Hill of Bush. If so, the car can be left about (480 812) and the Cooran Lane forded near where the Cornarroch Strand comes in from the west. A direct ascent from here—steep zigzags make it easier—takes you to Snibe Hill. The walk along the top is over great granite slabs with perched boulders and little pools to the cairn on Craignaw. The descent from here to the north-west is steep and needs care. It is best to go down a hollow between the rocks, aiming at the conspicuous cairn in the col. From here a descent is made due east. Before descending, look for the track across the flat ground going more or less straight for the cottage at Back Hill of Bush. The route lies between the Round and Long Lochs of the Dungeon and goes across the floating bog of the 'Silver Flow' which is now a Nature Reserve. If the track is followed this is not unduly wet, but care is needed. The road is followed for some 2 miles back to the car. The route may be reversed without any difficulty. (6-7 miles.) The new footbridge of No.23 may now be used instead of fording the river.

14   Dungeon Hill (2000 ft) and Loch Enoch   NC*

As in No. 13, if permission is obtained have a car at Back Hill of Bush. Cross the Silver Flow, aiming for the cairn and from the cairn climb the slopes of Dungeon Hill on the right. From it a descent to the sandy bays of Loch Enoch is easy. A return may be made from the south-east corner of Loch Enoch, over a small rise and down to the cairn in the col; from there back across the Silver Flow to Back Hill of Bush. (6-7 miles.)

15   Glenhead Lochs, Rig of the Jarkness   TNPRC*

Leave car at the car park near the Bruce Stone at Loch Trool. Walk up the road past Glenhead to the second burn coming down on the left (435 797). Follow the right branch of this burn for about a mile to the Round Loch. It is a pleasant walk round this, and across to the Long Loch, and then round the end of the Rig of the Jarkness to the east end of Loch Valley. Or, from the Round Loch climb east to Craiglee and follow the ridge north-west over the Rig of the Jarkness and down to Loch Valley. Follow the path from here down the Gairland Burn back to Buchan. (7 miles over Craiglee.)

16   Ben Yellary (2360 ft) and Merrick (2770 ft)   PNPC*

Leave a car at the car park near the Bruce Stone at Loch Trool and take the path up the west side of the Buchan Burn to Culsharg. Go straight north from there to the top of Ben Yellary and follow the dyke up the slope of the Merrick and so to the cairn. This is on the edge of the steep slopes to the Black Gairy Corrie to the north, and in poor weather care is needed. An easy descent can be made east to Loch Enoch, and the return journey made from its south-west corner due south to the burn running into Loch Neldricken. Visit this, and the 'Murder Hole' if desired, but the return route continues to the west of it, due south and comes down to the path beside the Gairland Burn. Again, if desired, a diversion east may be made to visit Loch Valley first. The path leads back to the road at Buchan (9-10 miles). In some ways this route is even better if followed in the reverse direction.

17   Kirriereoch (2565 ft) and Tarfessock (2282 ft)   TNTC*

From Newton Stewart follow A714 to Bargrennan and fork right up the Straiton Road for abut 7 miles (357 866). A track to the right through Kirriereoch Farm leads north-east to the Pillow Burn which can be followed on to the west slopes of Kirriereoch Hill and up the long ridge to the top. From the top, a descent is made to the north to Carmaddie Brae and past numerous pools to Tarfessock. A descent by the west ridge, and then turning south, leads back to the Pillow Burn and so to the roadend of the start. (10-11 miles.)

18   Shalloch on Minnoch (2522 ft) and Tarfessock (2282 ft)   TNTC*

Follow the Straiton Road as in No. 17 to Rowantree Junction (353 905) and go down the track on the right, across the bridge and up past Shalloch on Minnoch (Farm). From there strike up the slopes, a little north of east, to the top of Shalloch on Minnoch. A descent south of about a mile takes you to the Nick of Carclach and a farther mile to the top of Tarfessock. Return by the west ridge, turning a little north to the Knocklach Burn and down by the outward route to Rowantree. (9-10 miles.)

19   Loch Doon to Loch Riecawr and Loch Macaterick   TNPC*

Take the A713 road from Castle-Douglas to Ayr. Shortly before Dalmellington take the side road on the left to Loch Doon. This road is itself very picturesque and can be followed to the bridge over the Carrick Lane near the south end of the loch. The forestry track on the north side of the Carrick Lane can be followed for some $2\frac{1}{2}$ miles to Loch Riecawr. This track has now been continued west and north towards Ballochbeatties and joins the Straiton Road at Stinchar Bridge. This would give a good cross-over route when the forest gates are open. The best route from here to Loch Macaterick is probably over the little hill of Maccallum down to Loch Macaterick. The old path from Tunskeen by way of Loch Fannie and the edge of the forest to Loch Doon is crossed near the loch, and this gives the best route back to Loch Doon; but this path is not shown on some recent O.S. maps. But the most picturesque part of Loch Macaterick is the bay at the south end under the steep slopes of Macaterick. (7-8 miles.)

20   Loch Doon to Mulwharchar (2270 ft)   TNC*

Leave car at Carrick Lane as in No. 19 and continue down the track past Starr towards Loch Head. Leave it before reaching the Gala Lane and go along the slopes towards Craig Mawhannal. The ground here is rought and the going tiring. Make for the north ridge of Hoodens Hill which gives better walking and follow it to the top. Continue south over the Lump of the Eglin, down a little, and then over The Tauchers to Mulwharchar. A descent of a mile to Loch Enoch can be made if desired. Return by much the same route. A diversion to the west across the Eglin Lane may be made before reaching the Black Garpel. The cave mentioned in S.R. Crockett's THE RAIDERS, Cave Macaterick, is supposed to be some 500 yards south-west of the junction of the Black Garpel with the Elgin Lane, but the entrance is now lost. (11-12 miles.)

21 Pulskaig Burn, Loch Enoch, Dungeon Hill, Silver Flow RNPC*

As in Nos. 13 and 14, leave a car at Back Hill of Bush. Walk on up the forestry road for some two miles to the watershed, where the road is close to the burn, the Gala Lane, opposite the point where the Pulskaig Burn comes down the steep ravine between Dungeon Hill and Mulwharchar. This ravine leads directly to Loch Enoch, although the burn does not come out from it. A return may then be made over Dungeon Hill, down to the col of No. 13 and back across the Silver Flow. From Dungeon Hill the curved flow lines of the water on the Silver Flow may sometimes be seen. The writer has been fortunate enough to make this circuit in ice and snow and to walk on the frozen surface of Loch Enoch. Distance, 6 miles.

22 Longer Through Walks or Cross-overs

For energetic hill walkers the following routes are suggested in outline. They have all been followed in the last 20 years by school parties aged from 12-18 years, as one-day outings, with transport at both ends.

1   Murray's Monument or Craigdews, Millfore, Curlywee, Lamachan, Caldons on Loch Trool.

2   Forrest Lodge, Corserine, Back Hill of Bush, Silver Flow, Craignaw, Loch Valley, Loch Trool.

3   Loch Doon, Mulwharchar, Loch Enoch, Loch Neldricken, Loch Valley, Loch Trool.

4   Loch Doon, Loch Macaterick, Shalloch on Minnoch, Tarfessock, Rowantree Junction.

5   Craigencallie, Loch Dee, Loch Narroch, Loch Neldricken, Loch Enoch, Kirriereoch Hill, Kirriereoch Farm, Straiton Road.

6   Craigencallie, Loch Dee, Snibe Hill, Craignaw, Loch Enoch, Merrick, Ben Yellary, Loch Trool.

7   Clenries, Rhinns of Kells, Carsphairn.

23 Three Bridges Walk RNPRC C

This surprising circuit has recently become possible with the building of two forestry footbridges. It can, even so, sometimes be rough and wet in parts. Leave a car at Craigencallie and walk along the forestry road towards Loch Dee for about 1½ miles to the concrete bridge on the right and cross the Dee by it. Turn left and follow the forestry road for about 1½ miles, crossing a side burn coming from the right. There are several rides on the left leading down to the river bank and it is not always easy to pick the correct one - perhaps someday a post will indicate 'bridge'! The turning off point is about (480810) This ride is a rough few hundred yards to the river bank and the footbridge. After crossing the bridge turn left and follow what there is of a track - not much - which curves to the right where the burn from Loch Dee joins the Dee and continue towards Loch Dee. A little before the loch is reached is the second footbridge. A grassy and usually wet path leads back to the main forestry road again in about ½ mile. Turn left for the remaining 2 miles back to Craigencallie. There are some attractive sandy beaches at the end of Loch Dee near the footbridge. This route has some of the best and most varied views in the district, but although only 6 or 7 miles in distance it can be rough and tiring. The circuit can also be done in the opposite direction if desired.

Alternative approach

If a key to the forestry gate has been obtained, the Queensway road may be left before reaching Clatteringhsaws at (567771) by the forestry road to Mid Garrary. Turn left before Mid Garrary and go through the forestry gate. After about 2 miles a concrete bridge over the Dee is reached. A car may be left here. The walk circuit may then be done, in either direction, from this starting point. This reduces the walking distance by some 2 miles.

★ ★ ★

This seems an appropriate place to refer to the fine feat of the late Mr M'Bain, of Ayr, the veteran hill rambler of Galloway, and author of that interesting book, THE MERRICK AND NEIGHBOURING HILLS. He had been up the Merrick innumerable times over a great number of years, and at the age of eighty-four he thought he would like to climb the hill again. He did so, but the hill clouded down; and, not content with the one attempt, he waited three days for better weather and went up again! This is a record to be proud of: and may all we lovers of hills have the love of them in our hearts to the end like him!

Loch Enoch, Merrick and Kirriereoch

Threave Castle

Huntsman's Monument

Turner's Monument

Martyr's Monument

Neilson's Monument

Old Orchardton Tower

Lennox Tower

Footbridge near Loch Dee

Footbridge over River Dee

SECTION 8
Region west of Loch Ken south of the Newton Stewart–New Galloway Road A712

1 Dornell Loch and the Kirk Road RTRC

Leave the car at Glenlochar Dam and walk 1½ miles up the road on the west side of the Dee. Turn left up a steep little road—the 'Kirk Road' which crosses the summit in about a mile and passes through a wood close to Dornell Loch on the right. Another half mile takes you to the road back to Glenlochar. Turn sharp left and follow the road downhill most of the way. (6-7 miles.)

2 Airie Hill (947 ft) and Loch Skerrow TNTC*

Turn off the road from Laurieston to New Galloway at Little Duchrae (666 689). Leave the car after about a mile at the junction where the private road starts. Take the track to the right here. This rough track winds over a rise and down to the railway track near Airie Farm. An ascent of Airie Hill can be made from here; and a descent from the top due west to Loch Skerrow halt, from where the old railway track may be followed back to Airie. Or, the trak may be followed to Loch Skerrow and the climb done in reverse. (7-8 miles.)

3 Airie and Stroan Viaduct TC

Follow the previous route to Airie. Turn right at the railway track and follow it over the viaduct and the river to New Galloway Station. A mile and a half back down the road brings you to Little Duchrae which is a convenient place to leave a car for this circuit. (6-7 miles.)

4 Stroan Loch and Cairn Edward Forest PT or TC

From New Galloway Station follow the railway track to Stroan Viaduct and descend, before crossing the river, to the track on the right. This track may be followed round the loch and on up the east side of the Dee. About 2½ miles from the viaduct a branch to the left goes over a bridge to Barneywater. From there forest roads lead south to Loch Skerrow and Gatehouse. The main track continues up the Dee and can be followed through to Clatteringshaws. It is sometimes open for cars, and is part of the old 'Raiders' Road'.

Returning down the Dee, a track on the left at Stroan Loch brings you back to the main road at Bennan, a mile north of New Galloway Station; or the track may be followed to the viaduct and then left, for half a mile. A path on the right at the edge of the wood, leads over the grass back to the Station.

As in other forest regions there are other tracks and paths that can be followed to make further walks.

5 Black Craig of Dee (or Cairnsmore of Dee) (1616 feet) NC*

When approaching New Galloway from the east, this rounded dark hill is conspicuous behind the village. Follow the Clattering-shaws road for some 3½ miles and leave the car just before reaching the older forest on the left. A rough walk up steep broken ground brings you to the summit. A return may be made by the same route. (3 miles.)

6 Loch Fleet and Fell of Fleet (1544 feet) TNTC*

Leave car below the dam at Clatteringshaws and take the forest road on the south side of the Dee, immediately after crossing the river. In ¼ mile fork right uphill. After about 4 miles, that is about half-way along Loch Grannoch, turn left uphill along a ride (547 698) aiming for a dip between the hills and in a little over half a mile reach Loch Fleet. From the north end of the loch a further half mile north-east takes you to the top of the Fell. The best way off, though rough, is probably north along the ridge aiming for one of the forest tracks not yet shown on the O.S. map, near Orchars; or a return may be made by the ascent route. (11-12 miles.)

7 Loch Fleet from Gatehouse TNTC

A car may be left just after passing under the Big Water of Fleet viaduct. Go past the, usually locked, gate and follow the road on the left. After ½ mile take the right branch uphill, north-east, and continue for another 2 miles. Here fork left round the hill of Benmeal on your left. The track winds round and up, finally disappearing about ½ mile south of Loch Fleet. Go due north from here to the loch, and go along its west side to a dyke and a dip on the left. from here a ride west takes you down to the track above Loch Grannoch. Turn left and follow this track back to the start. Distance, about 8 miles.

8 Clatteringshaws to Gatehouse   TPT(X)

If transport can be arranged, this makes one of the best through-walks in the region. Follow the track as in 6 above, but continue until near the south end of Loch Grannoch. Cut down the half mile to the beach at the south end. This is a beach of clean sand, with the trees round the Lodge in the background and is an ideal picnic spot. From there follow the rough track through the gap to the south (the Cleugh of Eglon) and where the forest track turns east leave it by a path (547 668) running down to the river. This path continues, though in parts rather soft, down to the viaduct. The forest road may be followed on the other side of the Dee, although it is a little longer. A car can be brought to the viaduct for a cross-over.

Other forest tracks branch off fron the one mentioned above, running roughly north-east towards Loch Skerrow and the bridge at Barneywater mentioned in No. 4. These could be used to give further circuits, and the railway track used also as a return route.

Permission may sometimes be obtained to take a car on to these roads from the viaduct.

9 Clints of Dromore and Cairnsmore of Fleet (2331 feet)   NC*

(i)   From the Big Water of Fleet viaduct in No. 7 a scramble can be had over the rocky Clints and then by striking across the moor the ridge of Cairnsmore may be reached. A cairn marks the top of the Knee of Cairnsmore, but it is another 2 miles to the main top at the north end of the ridge. The distance is slightly less if a start is made from the old Gatehouse Station. 11 miles there and back.

(ii)   If transport is available, a return may be made from the cairn at the Knee down the long south-west ridge to the track end at Clanery and the track followed to Creetown (11 miles).

(iii)   An even better cross-over is to continue from the main top of Cairnsmore north-east, down and up to Meikle Mulltagggart. Continue north for about 1 mile to a cairn before turning north west over a rather boggy section and on to Craignelder. The ridge of this hill should be followed more or less north towards Murray's Monument. It is possible to ford the river just below the monument (or sometimes to wade). Distance from Gatehouse Station to Murray's Monument, about 11 miles.

Cairnsmore of Fleet from Corwar

(iv)   Another approach to Cairnsmore is from Talnotry Cottage on the road near Murray's Monument (476 706). A path leads down diagonally for about a mile to the river near Corwar where a bridge crosses the Palnure Burn; or a mile farther on a forest track leads down to the same bridge. A track leads up into the corrie — Deer's Den, and the north-west ridge of Cairnsmore reached easily. A short distance north of the top the remains of a German bomber from the 1941 attacks may be found. (9 miles.)

10   Loch Whinyon   NC

Take the road over the hill from Laurieston to Gatehouse. A little beyond the summit (612 623) a car can be left, and a slight ascent in a south-east direction leads in about a mile to Loch Whinyon. From the west end of the loch a path leads west down directly to the road again about a mile from where the car was left. (3½ miles.)

11   Loch Mannoch   PC

A car may be taken up the road from just west of Twynholm on the A75 to Glengap (652 595), where a car may be left. From the right turn at Glengap there is a pedestrian right-of-way which bypasses Lairdmannoch Lodge and leads round the east side of the loch to the Martyr's Monument (667 559). From there the right-of-way path leads past Kirkconnell to the A762 road from Ringford to Laurieston. Alternatively, it is a pleasant walk up the east side of the loch and back by the path down the west side, passing an old cairn and standing stone to make a circuit of some 4-5 miles.

12   Glengap Hill   TC

Car as in No. 11 to Glengap. Walk up track between Dow Craig on right and Fore Hill on left. After half a mile take the left fork. The track winds up, down and round the hillside returning to the road a half mile south of Glengap, and gives some very good views. (4 miles.)

CROSS-OVERS:

(i)   Starting as above at Glengap, if the right fork is taken a forest track leads on for some 6 miles, and emerges on the road from Laurieston to Gatehouse about 2 miles above Laurieston. This is a fine open walk. (8 miles Glengap t Laurieston.)

(ii)   Starting as above, about 2 miles from Glengap the road is only about ¼ mile from Loch Whinyon which can be reached by a sidetrack to it. The loch edge can be followed—though rough, to the path on the opposite side (as in No. 10) leading down to the Lurieston-Gatehouse road. (4 miles Glengap to Laurieston road.)

13   Cairharrow Hill (1496 feet)   NC*

Follow A75 to Skyreburn Bay and turn up the road on the right for 2 miles to Whiteside (554 565). From here a direct line takes you to the top in 1½ miles. With suitable transport, a return may be made westward down to the track at Claughreid and down it to the A75 at the Kirkdale bend (517 531). (Whiteside to Kirkdale, about 5 miles.)

14   Ravenshall, Dirk Hatteraick's Cave   PNPC

Coming from Gatehouse towards Ravenshall on the A75 a car may, with care, be left about (525 523) near a cottage. A path leads down through the trees to the rocks on the shore. Turn right on the shore for some ¼ mile — the going is very rough. The cave is up to the right and is not very easy to find — there is no obvious big opening. The entrance is in a little 'bay' and is a slit down a muddy slope between rocks. The slit opens out after some 10 feet and goes into the first chamber. There are several connected sections, with big flat surfaces reputed to be for sleeping on, and many smaller hollowed-out niches. Good torches are essential; a rope is useful for getting in and out by the slit, and it is probably better to leave one person outside with the end of the rope. Old clothes are advisable and anyone with well developed hips may have difficulty with the entrance slit!

15   Cairnholy   RC

The two ancient chambered cairns of Cairnholy are easy to visit from the coast road A75 from Gatehouse to Creetown. A car may be left where the road crosses the Kirkdale Burn, about 6 miles west of Gatehouse. Walk up the track towards Cairnholy Farm for about a mile. The cairns are just below the farm, on opposite sides of the road, and are reputed to be the finest examples of their kind in Galloway. Distance, 2 miles.

16   Gatehouse, Corse of Slakes Road, Creetown   RTR(X)

This walk follows the route of an old military road over the hills. Leave Gatehouse by the road to Gatehouse Station and turn left after ½ mile to Anwoth. At Anwoth turn right up the old track which goes up over a rise and down to meet, after 2½ miles, a road on the left coming up from Skyreburn Bay. Continue north-west and downhill by the Balloch Burn into Creetown. A bus can be used to return to Gatehouse. Distance, about 9 miles.

17   Laurieston Forest Walks   TC

(i)   South of the road from Laurieston to Gatehouse.
Leave the road at (653 652) by the forestry track on the south side. After about a mile fork left; the track goes near the edge of the forest and gives glimpses through the gaps towards Loch Mannoch. The track curves east and then north to Cullenoch; about ½ mile before Cullenoch take the left fork. The road is regained shortly after Cullenoch, and about a mile left, uphill brings you back to the start. Distance, about 5-6 miles.
(ii)   North of the road.
Take the track north at (647 651), beside some ruined buildings.

After a dip and rise take the left fork marked to Slogarie. This track goes round by the side of Lochenbreck Loch and then curves right round to Tormollan Hill, becoming faint and finally disappearing. Slogarie Farm can be seen about a mile to the north-east and is easily reached if it is desired to make a cross-over to the roadend of No. 2 at Little Duchrae. If not, a return can be made by the same track to the start.

(iii)   North of the road and round Kenick Hill.

Start as in (ii) above but do not fork left to Lochenbreck. At the next fork go left. The track twists up and down and round, curving east then south and after some 3 miles passes the junction to Summerhill on the left. Continue south for about another mile to regain the road at a large clearing with huts and turn right uphill for 1½ miles back to the start. Distance, about 5-6 miles.

18   Gatehouse – Dow Craig   RTC

From Gatehouse take the road north to Barlay Mill, about a mile out, where the road forks, and take the fork to the right. Less than half a mile beyond, take a minor road to the right, which runs into and up the fine glen of the Barlay Burn, crossing over the watershed and running away through the hills towards Loch Mannoch. Before reaching the latter, at Dow Craig Hill, the road swings round to the right, down the glen between Dow Craig and Fore Hill of Glengap. The road now runs south for a couple of miles to the farm of Trostrie, and a little beyond take the next road to the right, up to the farm of Carse; beyond which it becomes a lesser road (marked 'Old Military Road' — how very military they must have been!) taking you, in about 3 miles, on to the main Twynholm—Gatehouse Road, where you turn right for Gatehouse. This is a route that takes you 'far from the madding crowd' indeed! Length, 11 miles.

19   Craignelder (1971 feet)   TNRC*

Craignelder is the prominent hill on the left as one approaches Murray's Monument from the east. A forestry track leaves the A712 road on the south side at about (522 732). This curves pleasantly round and up the slopes of Craignarget and gives a good view east down to Loch Grannoch. Continue south-west up the rounded ridge to the cairn on Craignelder, from where fine views to the west are to be had. A return may be made directly down the slope towards

Murray's Monument, where the burn is forded or waded to reach the road 1½ miles from the start. Distance, about 5½ miles.

20   Loch Skerrow   NC*

This remote loch is at the highest part of the old railway line between New Galloway and Gatehouse Stations. It can be reached in several ways:

(i)   The shortest route is from the south. Leave the moor road from Laurieston to Gatehouse near its summit at (616 627) where a track goes off north. It may be possible to take a car for 1½ miles along this to the farm of Grobdale of Girthon and leave it there. Continue north by well marked sheep tracks. It is better going on the hillside rather than nearer the burn on the dotted path marked on the map. The sheep tracks lead past some big boulders from which the loch can be seen ½ mile ahead. The going is rough. Distance, 2½ miles.

(ii)   A car may be left at the forestry gate near the Big Water of Fleet Viaduct (560 646) and either the old railway track, or a forestry track roughly parallel may be walked. Distance, 3½ miles.

(iii)   A car may be left near Slogarie (652 689), ½ mile from the A762 road from Kirkudbright to New Galloway. A farm track is then followed for some 2 miles to Airie Farm and then the old railway track to the loch. Distance, about 3½ miles.

(iv)   On certain days the Forestry Commission allows cars on the road up the Dee from Mossdale to Clatteringshaws. At a point some 3 miles from Mossdale (622716) a forestry track crosses the river by a bridge at Barneywater and continues south-west for some 3 miles to Loch Skerrow.

With some suitable arrangements for transport a combination of two of the above routes would give a pleasantly varied walk.

21   Loch Grannoch Lodge   TC

Start as in No. 7 to Loch Fleet. At the junction after half a mile take the left fork and follow some signs to Loch Grannoch Lodge always keeping to the left. After 2½ miles the track enters the ravine. 'The Cleugh of Eglon' and climbs up steeply to the watershed. This gives the first view of Loch Grannoch. At the summit there is a memorial tablet to a pony. Half a mile downhill on the track takes you to the trees beside the lodge, which is now an outdoor centre.

The best beach is over to the right, before going along the path to the lodge.
N.B. It is possible to go from the beach up over a very rough piece of moor and join the track of No. 7 that comes south from Clatteringshaws. Walk to lodge and back, about 6 miles.

22   Muncraig Shore and Ringdoo   NC

Leave the coast road B727 west of Kirkudbright at Borgue and go left for half a mile to the second road on the left to High Chapelton and Muncraig; A car may be left near Muncraig. Permission should be sought at Muncraig to go across to the coast near Ringdoo Point and Bay. There are several caves and good cliff scenery, but access to the caves is difficult unless the tide is very low. Distance Muncraig to shore, about 1 mile.

23   Bombie Glen from Kirkcudbright   RC

For this road walk leave Kirkcudbright by the B727 road from the town centre. After about half a mile, at a sharp bend where the B727 goes sharply left, go straight on by a tarred road to Kirkland. This, after a mile brings you down to the picturesque valley of the Buckland Burn. At the bridge (703499) turn left and continue uphill, on the same side of the burn for some 2 miles to Whinnie Liggate. On the way you are looking across to Bombie and the attractive Bombie Glen. At Whinnie Liggate turn left down the B727 again into Kirkcudbright. Distance about 6-7 miles.

24   Threave Castle   RP

This ancient pre-15th century castle was for many years the seat of the Black Douglases. It is situated on an island in the river Dee a little west of Castle Douglas, and is still an impressive ruin. It is under the care of the National Trust for Scotland and can be reached only by boat from a jetty at the end of the access road. A signpost on the A75 a mile west of Castle Douglas indicates the access road past Kelton Mains to a small car park. There is then about a mile of well made path to the ferry jetty. It is possible at times to be rowed over to the castle. Distance 1 mile each way.

SECTION 9
The Region bounded by the Nith Valley on the west, the road to Wanlockhead and Leadhills B797, and the Moffat Road A701

1 Kettleton Reservoir TPTC

From Thornhill station take the road sharp left, then very sharp back right and then up a long straight hill. This road leads round to Mitchell Slacks and back to Ae village or Closeburn, and gives access to many of the hill walks in this region.

At Burn Farm (904 981) leave a car and go up a track on the left. This leads after about 1½ miles to the reservoir, a pleasant picnic spot. It is possible, but rough going, to walk round it. At the dam end, some 150 feet up on the right, a path leads round the slopes of Par Hill and joins a track through the hills from Durisdeer to Garroch. In half a mile leave the track again (916 011) for a path running south into the deep cleft of Cample Cleuch. This path leads back to Burn. (6 miles.)

2 Auchenleck Hill (1466 feet) NPRC*

Leave the road described in the last note at its highest point (934 975) and go up the slopes to the north. A gentle walk of a mile or so brings you to the summit above a very small lochan. Continuing north, a descent over steep slopes can be made to the White Snout and a return to the road by turning left and down Cample Cleuch. The road is followed back to the car. (6½-7 miles.)

3 Gana Hill (2191 feet) N*

This may be approached from the Mitchell Slacks road (1, above) from three directions, any two of which will give a circular walk.

(i) Leave road at bridge (942 977) and walk up past Garroch. Turn left and go up the slopes of Tod Craig Hill and on up the gradual ridge to Gana. (3½ miles to top.)

(ii) Leave road at Locherben (957 970) and go up the slopes on the left to a cairn (Crichton's Cairn). Continue due north up the ridge over Hard Hill to Gana. (4 miles to top.)

(iii)   Leave road at Mitchell Slacks (965 961), cross the bridge and follow the track up the east side of the Capel Burn for some three miles. Cross this burn where the Campbell Cleuch Burn comes in from the west, and go up the slopes on its right, turning gradually left to the summit. (5 miles to top.)

4   Earncraig Hill (2000 feet) and Penbreck (1998 feet)   TNTC*

Start from Mitchell Slacks as in iii but continue straight on to the slopes of Earncraig Hill which blocks the glen ahead. A path leads up to the pass on the west. From the watershed on the west turn right for the summit. A good view to the Daer reservoir is got from the ridge here in a north-east direction. After half a mile cut across to the slope of Penbreck and follow it south to the top. From here, keeping south for half a mile, a side burn may be followed westward to the track back to Mitchell Slacks. (11-12 miles.)

5   Queensberry (2286 feet)   TNTC*

(i)   From Mitchell Slacks as in the previous section. Follow the track for some 2½ miles until approaching New House (973 988) and bear up the slope to the right. This rises gently, and not very interestingly, to the top in about 1½ miles. A more interesting descent can be made towards Wee Queensberry, below which the ground is cut into some deep rocky hollows. From here take the south-west slope back to the track about a mile north of Mitchell Slacks. (7 miles.)

(ii)   From Beattock. RTNCA car can be taken to Kinnelhead and a track followed for a mile to Lochanhead. Cross the burn here and turn west up the slopes of Lamb Hill so to Queensberry, keeping just north of the present forest edge. (8 miles.)

(iii)   From Branrigg. If access through the Ae Forest is allowed, this makes an attractive route. From Ae Village follow the Loch Ettrick Road for ½ mile and turn down sharp right. The road winds up the picturesque glen of the Water of Ae for some 3 miles to a bridge. Beyond this the road is usually closed to cars, but may be walked. After about 2½ miles turn down sharp left, cross the Ae again and and go up past Branrigg and continue to the end of the road. A fire break about here gives access to the hill towards Wee Queensberry and so to Queensberry. From the gate to Queensberry and back is about 14 miles. This route could be combined with one of the others by a suitable arrangement for transport.

6   Ae Forest

This large tract of forest extends for about 7 miles north to south and about 5 miles east to west, and is roughly pear shaped with the apex at Queensberry and the centre of the 'base' at Ae Village. The road to Ae Village turns off the Dunfries-Moffat road at Ae Bridgend (011 868) and runs through the forest to Loch Ettrick, where the left branch goes back to Closeburn on A76 and the right branch continues through the forest to Mitchell Slacks. Easy access to the forest can be got from several places on this road.

(i)   AE VILLAGE. Take track to left at crossroads. This branches after ¼ mile and gives several round walks.

(ii)   AE VILLAGE. Turn sharp right downhill, cross bridge and then turn either left or right.

(iii)   Half a mile up the Loch Ettrick road past Ae, turn sharp right downhill and follow road to Branrigg.

(iv)   Two miles up from Ae turn right and cross to Gubhill from where several tracks lead into the forest.

(v)   From the Moffat Road, half a mile past Bridgend, turn left (017 877) for one mile to Townhead. A track on the right leads up to the east side of the Glenkiln Burn.

(vi)   From the road between Loch Ettrick and Mitchell Slacks several tracks lead into the forest.

Many of the tracks mentioned can be linked to give short or long circuits as desired. The Forestry Commission has published more detailed notes on some of the walks in this forest.

7   Scaw'd Law (2167 feet) and Glenleith Fell (2003 feet)   TNTC*

From Durisdeer follow the track south-east towards Glenaggart. Just after crossing the Glenimp Burn strike up the hillside north-east to Blackgrain Shoulder and on to Scaw'd Law. A gentle descent and rise for about 1 mile south brings you to Glenleith Law. From here a descent south-west brings you back to the track through Glenaggart and so back to Durisdeer. (5-6 mile.)

8   Wedder Law (2186 feet)   TNTC*

From Duisdeer follow the Glenaggart track for some 3 miles to the watershed. Cross Glenleith Burn and turn left up the ridge of the Wedder Law. A further mile north-east is the small subsidiary top of

Shiel Dod giving a good view down towards the Daer reservoir. (To Wedder Law and back, 10 miles; including Shiel Dod, 12 miles.)

These two hills may also be climbed by approaching from the north (NC). From the Dalveen Pass road (A702) about 4 miles south of Elvanfoot, turn across the river by the Daer reservoir road. Follow it down the west side to Kirkhope. From there the hill slopes up south-west and over Ewe Gair to Shiel Dod and Weddder Law. (6 miles from Kirkhope.)

9 Mitchell Slacks to Daer TPT(X)

A good through-walk can be made by linking up the approach from Mitchell Slacks to Earncraig Hill (No. 4) with the Daer road. From the watershed west of Earncraig Hill, continue northwards downhill and cross to a track on the left leading to Daer. (Mitchell Slacks to Kirkhope, 8-9 miles.)

10 Ballencleuch Law (2268 feet) and Rodger Law (2258 feet) TNTC*

Park car near the watershed on the Dalveen Pass road (A702). A track from Troloss or a path half a mile east lead down to the Roman Road to Durisdeer. Follow this for about 2 miles to near its watershed and then turn east. Go up the slopes on the south of Gana Burn to Ballencleuch Law. From there an easy mile north-east takes you to Rodger Law. From there the return is best made for a mile due west before swinging north and descending to the track and back to the Dalveen road. (8-9 miles.) As in No. 9 these two hills can now be reached conveniently from the Daer reservoir road to Kirkhope.

11 Lowther Hill (2387 feet) to Dun Law (2216 feet) RNTRC*

Park car at Wanlockhead and walk up the road to Lowther Hill. Continue east to Green Lowther (2403 feet), where the road ends. Continue north-east over a smaller hill t Dungrain Law. A dip and ascent brings you to Dun Law. From here a long slope north-west and then west leads into the upper part of the glen of the Shortcleuch Burn. A track north leads down to the road a mile east of Leadhills, but it is shorter to continue due west and reach the road in the village of Leadhills itself. (Distance, 9-10 miles.) This route, or part of it, is invigorating in early spring when the whole view is of snow-covered hills; but care must be taken as some of the slopes are steep.

12   Roman Road or Well Path, to Durisdeer   T(X)

Go to the summit of the Dalveen road A702 near Troloss, as in No. 10. Follow the track down to the right and turn south after about a mile at some sheep pens. The track goes south-west between Well Hill on the right and Durisdeer Hill on the left, to a watershed at about 1300 ft and then down the side of the Kirk Burn to Durisdeer. Continue on the road for another mile past Durisdeer back to the Dalveen road, at (884 022). If a car is left at this junction a bus may be taken to the starting point. The church in the picturesque village of Durisdeer contains the famous Queensberry Memorial marbles which may usually be inspected. Distance, 5½ miles.

13   Dalveen, Enterkin, Mennock – a glen walk   TPNRPNTC

This and the following walk, No. 15, are in the same region, but whereas this one keeps to the glens and is longer the other goes over the tops and is higher, steeper and more exposed to the weather.

Leave a car at a lay-by just past the roadend to Nether (or Lower) Dalveen at (886 067) and walk up the track past the farm buildings. The track winds up steeply in an attractive tree-filled glen and after the top twists left and down to the Enterkin track. Turn right and follow this old bridle-path—marked by posts—for two miles uphill to the gap between Lowther Hill on the right and East Mount Lowther on the left (west) side. (The author is not responsible for the naming!) This gap is at about 1750 ft. Here, leave the path, turn left and go down steeply, a little north of west, for about ½ mile to the road in the Mennock Pass. Turn left down the road for about ½ mile to (866 101) where a path goes off on the left and inclines up the hillside; this is 'Dempster Road' and it curves up and round the hillside for about a mile, gradually turning south and coming down to Glenim. Here turn east and make for the dip above Nether Dalveen which can be seen in the distance, about 2 miles away. A good path goes from Glenim for a mile east; after that the hillside to the north of the Auchenlone Burn is very rough and it is probably easier to come along the south-west side, crossing the deep drop at the junction with the Enterkin Burn and so back to Dalveen. Distance, 8 miles.

Well Hill and Dalveen Pass

Enterkin Pass and Lowther Hill

14   Steygail, Lowther Hill, East Mount Lowther   TNTC*

This walk takes you over the tops of the hills in what can be one of the windiest parts of south Scotland. In wintry weather the walker must be prepared for violent winds and conditions of extreme cold. Start as in No. 13 but at the crest above the little wood turn right and go up the gentle grassy slope eastward on to Steygail, with fine views all around, especially to the north. The walker should now go north-east down the grassy slope for some 300 ft to the, usually sheltered, little col. From here turn due north up the long 1½ miles over Wether Hill to the Radio Station on the summit of Lowther Hill (2378 ft). From here do not follow the road, but go down west, to the left of the road, curving gradually round to the crest of the Enterkin Path with its posts. Cross the Enterkin Path here and go up, in a direction a little west of south, on to East Mount Lowther (2069 ft) and on south over Thirstane Hill for some 2 miles to the junction of the Enterkin and Auchenlone Burns. From there return by the track as in No. 13 to Dalveen. Note that two rounded ridges run south from Thirstane Hill; it does not matter which is taken. Distance, 6-7 miles, but some 2500 ft of ascents.

15   Lowther Hill and Green Lowther from Dalveen Pass   NRNC

For this walk a car can be left near the summit of the Dalveen Pass near Troloss (about 910 083) at some 1000 ft. Go due north on to Comb Head (1999 ft) and then north-west over Cold Moss. A small dip and then a rise brings you in a little over two miles from the road to the top of Lowther Hill (2378 ft). Here turn right, in a north-east direction, along the road that goes for a mile and a half to the masts on the summit of Green Lowther (2404 ft), the highest point in the Lowther Hills. From here continue north-east for another ½ mile to a small, unnamed round bump and then go south-east down the long rounded shoulder of Riccart Law Rig, over a little top (1786 ft) and so down to the road south of Nether Fingland. This is some 2 miles from the start. Distance, 7-8 miles.

16   Other Lowther tops: Dungrain Law, Dun Law, Lousie Wood
   Law   NC*

These three tops lie to the east of those in Nos 14 and 15. Leave a car on the Dalveen to Elvanfoot road (A702) a little north of

Glenochar at about (951 139) and go north-west on to Coupland Gair (1686 ft). Continue north-west to the rounded top of Lousie Wood Law (2028 ft). Here turn south-west, dipping down for half a mile and then up again over White Law (1982 ft). After another mile the top of Dun Law (2216 ft) is reached. Still going south-west, another sharp dip and rise brings you to Dungrain Law (2187 ft) in about half a mile. From here make a steepish descent in a direction a little south of east, crossing the Big Windgate Burn after about a mile and continuing on the north side of the Peden Burn, past a little reservoir and so back to the road about a mile south of the start. Distance, about 7 miles.

17   Durisdeer, Black Hill, Well Hill, Durisdeer   NTC*

Turn off the Dalveen Pass road (A702) at the junction at (884 022) and continue to Durisdeer, where a car may be left (see No. 13). Go through the village and cross the burn towards the hill immediately north of it. Continue due north up the slopes of Black Hill for 1½ miles to its top. Here turn east and go down a little for some ½ mile from the top, then up again in a north-easterly direction over a subsidiary top and on to the summit of Well Hill after another mile. From the Cairn on Well Hill turn right (south-east) and go down beside the boundary wall to the watershed on the Well Path. Turn right and return by the track to Durisdeer. Distance, about 5½ miles.

18   Wanlockhead, Stood Hill, Black Hill   RTNC*

A car may be left at Wanlockhead on the B7040 road from Mennock to Elvanfoot. Walk up the road through the village that goes north-west, past old mine workings, and soon becomes a track. About 1½ miles from the village, a path goes off on the left up the slopes of Glengaber Hill (1690 ft). Leave this path before the summit and go south-east along the high broad ridge, with a small dip, towards Stood Hill (1926 ft) in about a mile. The ridge now undulates over several bumps in a more or less south-east direction to the top of Black Hill. This is immediately above the village and gives a fine view across to the main tops of the Lowther Hills. Distance, about 4½ miles.

19   Loch Lurkie and Falbae Moor   RTRC

Follow the A713 road north from Castle-Douglas for about 5 miles to a road junction on the right at about (718 689) near Parton Mill House. Go up this road for about a mile to a fork at

Barwhillanty; a car may be left near here. Walk up the right fork, passing Loch Lurkie on the left, among attractive clumps of trees. After another quarter of a mile turn left at the edge of the forest along a forestry track. In ½ mile this enters Falbae Forest and divides into three; the left and centre branches combine again after about three-quarters of a mile, so either can be followed. After they rejoin, another ¼ mile brings you to a metalled road running south-west. Turn left and follow this for 1½ miles to a junction near Mid Laggan. Turn left again downhill and in another 1½ miles return to the starting point. Distance, about 5½ miles. There are three small lochs hidden in the trees, if you can find them!

Falbae Loch frozen over

20   Crichope Linn   NC

Crichope Linn is a remarkable sandstone gorge cut by the burn that flows into the Cample Water some 2 miles east of Thornhill. It can be reached by turning off the A76 road at Closeburn, over the railway, and in a quarter of a mile turning left. After about 2 miles the road is running alongside a burn on the right, which soon bears away from the road, on the right, and diappears into the trees. A few hundred yards past this point is an old quarry where a car may be left. Go back towards the burn, but before reaching it turn left along a dyke and go up the left side of this dyke, keeping outside the trees. Where the ground levels off after some hundreds of yards a stile over the wall leads to a path and this to broad sandstone steps that go down to the gorge. The steps are damp and slippery and it is better to visit the place in dry weather and before the summer growth of grasses, ferns and brambles obscures the route. About half-way down the path branches and the left branch goes left through a little natural tunnel to give a sensational view up the gorge. The whole place is like a miniature 'Grand Canyon'. The right branch of the path continues down, in a slippery fashion, to the water's edge and it is possible to continue down on that side back to the road, or to cross the burn and go down the other side to the road. Caution is needed throughout the approach, especially if children are present. The paths have been greatly improved by voluntary local work.

Distance, perhaps a mile there and back.

21 Watchman's Clump   RTNC*

From many places in the neighbourhood of Dumfries people looking towards Queensberry can see a small clump of trees on a rounded hillslope to the south of Queensberry. The hillslope is the Watchman's Moor and the trees form the Watchman's Clump. A visit to them is a pleasant walk with good open views. The back road from Heathhall to Dalswinton is followed. Turn right at Duncow; a car may be taken for about 1½ miles uphill from there and left near a sharp corner at Whitehall. A track goes north on to the moor and a line is followed to the now obvious clump of trees ahead. Returning a route further east can be taken to the east corner of a belt of trees and on to a track leading down to Ellerslee and by turning right at the first junction back to Whitehall. Distance, 3½ miles.

22 Dalswinton Loch   RC

This picturesque little loch is celebrated as the site of the trials of the first steamboat, built by Patrick Miller of Dalswinton in 1788. It may be seen from an adjoining public road although the path round it is private. The loch lies just south of the back road from Heathhall to Auldgirth on the north side of the Nith, and lies between the road and the river. A car may usually be left near the houses at Dalswinton (937854) about a mile south of Auldgirth or about 5 miles from Heathhall. A narrow road goes straight down opposite the houses towards the river and then left, continuing near the river. It goes left again past some farm buildings and then past the end of the loch. The road continues left again to rejoin the Heathhall Auldgirth road about a mile from the start. Hence, if desired, a circuit may be made, or a return by the original route to Dalswinton. Distance about 3 miles round.

It may be possible to obtain permission to walk round the loch which is very attractive and has many fine trees near it.

23   The Barony and Nethermill   RC

This is a flat but pleasant road walk on fairly quiet roads. A car may be left near the road junction at (017 875) near Parkgate on the A701 to Moffat. Here turn right between the houses and it is usually permitted to follow the road past The Barony School with its picturesque little lochs and so on to the road from Parkgate. Turn right along the road for a mile, then left for a mile past Gamerigg to the Nethermill junction. Here turn left again and in about 2 miles reach Parkgate. Half a mile along the busy A701 brings you back to the start. Distance about 6 miles.

24   Elshieshields, Cumrue, Hazliebrae   RC

This is a short but varied walk on quiet country roads. Leave Lochmaben by the north road B7020 but fork left before reaching the old railway and go past the Mill Loch. After about a mile the tower of Elshieshields above the Water of Ae is passed and the river crossed. A car may be left at the junction here (066 852). Go north for half a mile to a cross road near Cumrue, turn left and go past Cumleys and then fork left. After crossing a burn turn left again (051 862) and go along a straight road above the river. This winds round past Hazliebrae and shortly returns to the starting point. Distance about 3 miles.

25   Ae Forest, Townhead, Glenkiln, Lamphitt   TNPTRC

This walk is indicated briefly in No. 6, v, P.92, and is now given with a circuit. A car may be left near Townhead (005 884). A track goes off on the right (north) and winds uphill, with picturesque views for some 2½ miles to the farm of Glenkiln. Shortly after this, at the end of a dyke on the left, a ride will be seen leading down to Glenkiln Burn where a tributary comes down from the west side. It is possible, but rough, to go down this and cross both burns. A path then leads up in a short distance to the forestry track on the west bank. After about a mile a clearing shows a track down left to Lamphitt and then round the hillside to the right and down to the road at Wood Farm. Turn left for a mile back to Townhead. Distance about 6 miles.

Comb Law

26   Dalveen, Meikle Shag, Comb Law   PNPRC*

On the Dalveen Pass road A702, a car may be left near Over Fingland at (927 092). This is just above a footbridge over the Portrail Water a quarter of a mile south. After crossing the bridge make straight up the steep slopes of Meikle Shag to its top (1646 ft) and continue in a south-westerly direction for another mile and a half, keeping near the dyke, to the top of Comb Law (2108 ft). A good view down to the Daer Reservoir is obtained by going a little down to the south-east from the top. The return can be made pleasantly by going south-west for half a mile and curving gradually to the right, descending to the obvious junction and footbridge at a little wood beside sheep pens. From there the old Roman Road leads back to the A702 and the starting point. Distance about 5 miles.

27 Carron Linn   TC

About 2 miles north of Carronbridge on the A702 at (881 012) on the east side. A very attractive short scenic walk. It is a nature trail along the river, with fine trees, flowers, birds and animals. See notice at start. A return is probably best made to the start, although it is possible to scramble up the bank and return by the road. Distance about 1 mile.

28 Morton Castle and Loch   RC

A car may be left at the road junction above the old Thornhill station (see ˙ Section 9, 1) Take the road by Manse Brae and Kirkland. After about a mile, straight uphill, turn left along another straight road for another mile. A gate and a grassy track lead down to the castle on its fine site above the little loch. Good views may be had from the low ground down to the right, but the ground on the other, west side is awkward to reach. The castle is reputed to be from the twelfth century and is an impressive ruin. Continue for about another mile past Morton Mains to a 4-way junction. Take the left most road here for some two miles back to the old station. This part of the road is open and gives fine views across the valley to Drumlanrig Castle. Distance about 4½ miles.

29 Drumlanrig Castle   Varied walks

From Thornhill take the Penpont road A702 across the Nith and then take the first road on the right. This runs for some two miles north, past the castle and comes back to the A76 after crossing Drumlanrig Bridge. Just before this bridge the castle drive curves left up to the castle. As well as the castle with its car park, refreshment facilities and adventure area and its art treasures the grounds have many miles of walks in the woods, with fine trees and some small lochs. There are both paved and grassy tracks. These may normally be walked even if the castle itself is not open to visitors. Distances - varied to suit.

30 Enterkin Track RPR

This walk takes you over a part of the track by the Enterkin Pass to Wanlockhead, at its south end. It gives fine open views over the Nith Valley and returns by the Dalveen road. Approach from Carron Bridge by the Dalveen Road A702. About 1½ miles after passing under the railway (882 035) a road goes off left. This is the start of the walk and a car may be left here. Follow this side road for ½ mile to a 4-way junction at Muiryhill. Turn right up a narrow road signposted Inglestone. In another ½ mile this road forks, the left fork going to Inglestone. At this junction is the official post and notice indicating the start of the Enterkin Track, a public footpath to Wanlockhead. Follow the right fork uphill, partly on a pleasant grassy track with fine views across the valley in the Sanquhar direction and views of the Lowther hills and the radar domes ahead. Hereabouts also is another section of the Deil's Dyke as shown on the older O.S. maps. After about 2 miles and before the track drops steeply towards Glen Valentine on the left, a track comes in from the right, from Nether Dalveen. Turn along this, a little uphill first then steeply down the picturesque glen past Nether Dalveen and so back to the A702 road again. Turn right for a final mile and a half back to the car. Distance about 6 miles.

31 Coshogle–Glenim Track RPR

This is an open moor walk in an unfrequented part of the hills. Turn off the A76 at Enterkinfoot (858043) by the road on the right, steeply uphill to Coshogle. Before reaching Coshogle, at a very sharp U bend, a car may be left. Walk back a few yards and take the farm track on the right which curves up to the finely situated farm of Kirkbride. A track starts from here going a little east of north over grassy slopes, crossing a burn by a stone bridge and continuing across the moor northwards to a cairn, Laydow Cairn, with wide open views. Just before the cairn another track from the south is met and this forms the return route. This track keeps on the easy side of the burn and heads towards the trees, keeping along a little below them to an obvious gap. It is now a forestry track and leads down to the houses at Coshogle. Turn right downhill to the U bend and the car. Distance about 4½ miles.

32 Deil's Dyke Walk   PNPR

This ancient rampart of turves and stones has been traced for some 50 miles from west to east, its origins being uncertain. The 4 mile section between Ulzieside, just south of Sanquhar, and above Glen Airlie Bridge was clearly shown on the older O.S. 1 : 50,000 and old 1-inch maps, but has been removed from the new 1987 series. It is however, fairly easy to pick out and follow on the ground. It follows roughly the contours at a height of about 900 feet, that is some 500 feet above the river Nith. Much of the intervening slope is forested and the approach is best made at the north, Sanquhar, end. Turn off the A76 at Sanquhar by the Euchan road and cross the Nith. Turn left immediately and go just past the farm at Ulzieside. A car may be left about here. Go back past the farm and follow the signs indicating the 'Southern Upland Way' for a bit uphill. After several styles or gates the 'way' track veers to the left and it is better to curve round the hillside a little more to the right on another, unmarked, track. As you approach the 900 feet level parts of the Dyke can be seen going off on the left. There is an electricity power line above in some places, below in others. The Dyke twists along the hillside for some 4 miles and ends about the stone dyke coming up from the Nith that marks the Parish boundary. The best route down from here, because of the forestry work, is to follow a forestry track that inclines down to Bournmouth, ½ mile south of Glen Airlie Bridge. From there it is some 4 miles on the road back to Sanquhar and Ulzieside. Distance 8 miles.

SECTION 10
The region east of the
Lockerbie–Moffat–Tweedsmuir roads
1   Moffat, Moffat Water, St. Mary's Loch

The road (A708) from Moffat to Selkirk up the glen of the Moffat Water is attractive all the way, and any part or all of it is worth walking over; but the road is narrow, hard and long, and at some times the traffic is too heavy for any pleasure in walking—at sunny weekends and in the summer months. Moffat to St. Mary's Loch, 16 miles; to Selkirk, a farther 18 miles. The views are probably better when walking up rather than down, and are particularly fine when the hills are snow-covered. By judicious use of car or bus a selected part of the route may be done on foot. The walks in the next sections go up some of the many, and sometimes very impressive, side glens and on to the surrounding hills.

2   Round Blackhope Glen. Saddle Yoke and Hart Fell   NC*

Proceed by car to Capplegill (144 097) some 5½ miles up the glen of the Moffat Water from Moffat, where a car may be left. Go up the slopes on the right, north side, over Peat Hill and on to Saddle Yoke. The summit ridge is narrow and the slopes are steep, but there is a path. Note that there are two tops, the first, south top 2413 ft, the second 2445 ft. From the north top descend gently north-west for ½ mile, then curve north and go on round the end of the burn on the left without descending any further, for about a mile. At the watershed here (133 142) turn south-west along the county boundary (fence), and go up over Hartfell Rig (2423 ft), then a small dip and on in a generally westerly direction, following the fence, to the top of Hart Fell (2651 ft). From here go south-east keeping near the edge of the steep slopes to Blackhope Glen, over a small top (2373 ft) and on past Swatte Fell. (The cairn is ½ mile away to the south-west.) Continue more or less south-east past Black Craig and down the steep slope back to Capplegill. Distance, about 8 miles plus some 3000 feet of ascents.

In snow conditions the ridge on Saddle Yoke can be exhilarating, but an ice axe should be carried—the snow slopes to the sides are very steep. For experienced climbers only, the ascent of the steep ridge of Black Craig from Blackhope Glen can give a good climb, especially in snow.

3   Round Carrifran Glen, Saddle Yoke and White Coomb   NC*

Start as in No. 2 over Saddle Yoke, but after the ½ mile descent north-west bear right and go along above the rocks of Raven Craig in a north-east direction, keeping along the county boundary fence for a bit. After a boggy section with the appropriate name of Rotten Bottom, follow the fence north and then east to the top of Firthhope Rig (2627 ft). There leave the helpful fence and go east, then south-east to the rounded top of White Coomb (2696 ft) in about ¾ of a mile. A descent may be made into the wide corrie on the Moffat Water side by going south-east from the cairn. There is a steep slope after leaving the cairn but this soon eases off and the road is reached some 3 miles up from the start. Distance, 9-10 miles.

4   Hart Fell and Swatte Fell   PNC*

The most direct route up Hart Fell is from the glen that runs north from Moffat, below the Beef Tub. When leaving Moffat branch right at the school and follow the road up the east side of the river for some 3 miles to a small hall on the roadside, where a car may be left. A few yards beyond this a gate gives access to a path that goes up the long rounded slopes on the north side of the Auchencat Burn. If going direct to Hart Fell, keep up the centre of this slope. If it is desired to visit the Chalybeate Well, keep along the edge of the burn for about 1½ miles to the well, and then scramble up steeply on the left to the crest of the ridge. The ridge continues over Arthur's Seat and then curves a little to the left to reach the Ordnance Pillar in about another mile. On the return, leave the top as in No. 2, but after the small top (2373 ft) continue near the edge until approaching Swatte Fell and bear right, south-west, to the cairn. From the cairn continue south-west over Blue Cairn and make for the starting hall at the roadside. It is probably better not to try to cross the Auchencat Burn on the way down. Distance, about 8½ miles.

5   Hart Fell from the Beef Tub Summit   N(X)*

This is an interesting, but longer, route to Hart Fell that takes advantage of the height of the Tweedsmuir road A701 above the Beef Tub to reduce the height to be climbed; but it is best combined with a part of one of the other routes 2, 3 or 4 above to make a cross-over, with the provision of suitable transport at the other end.

Grey Mare's Tail

Take a car to the top of the Beef Tub and about ½ mile farther; here a clearing on the right can be used to leave a car (055 128). Go up the ridge to the north for ½ mile to the small top of Annanhead Hill (1566 ft) where the county boundary fence is met. The route follows this boundary fence up and down over a series of tops—Great Hill, Chalk Rig Edge, Spout Craig, Barry Grain Rig—and a final ascent of a mile to the top of Hart Fell. Distance from the road to the top, about 5 miles. A return may be made as in No. 4 to the hall on the low road, by either side of the Auchencat Burn; or as in No. 2 down the south side of the Blackhope Glen to Capplegill; or by the outward route of No. 2 over Saddle Yoke and down to Capplegill. The last is probably the best expedition, but the longest (about 10-11 miles).

6   Round Loch Skeen, Lochcraig Head and White Coomb   PNC*

Leave a car at the car park at the National Trust area at the foot of the Grey Mare's Tail Burn and go up by the path on the north-east side of the burn. Note the warnings displayed by the National Trust and take great care on these slopes. The writer has, on separate occasions, seen a dog and a sheep lose their footholds and roll uncontrollably down these slopes of what looks like innocent grass. Above the falls keep on the north-east side, along past Loch Skeen, a little up from the water's edge. The boundary fence may help to get over the boggiest parts here. Continue in a north-west direction straight up the slopes of Lochcraig Head to the top (2625 ft). From it go south-west down a little and then up to Firthybrig Head (2504 ft), then on south-west over the bump of Donald's Cleuch Head to Firthhope Rig (2627 ft). Here, as in No. 3, turn and go a little south of east to White Coomb and descend to the road as in No. 3, reaching it a little below the car park. Distance, 6-7 miles.

7   Hills on the East side of the Moffat Water–Herman Law to Bell Craig   PNRC*

A car may be taken to the summit at Birkhill of the A708 road from Moffat to Sellkirk, where the county boundary crosses the road. This makes a good starting point, the boundary fence acting as a guide for about a mile up the slopes east to the top of Herman Law (2014 ft). From here it is a pleasant walk south-west over the tops of

Trowgrain Middle (2058 ft), Mid Rig (2114 ft), Andrew-whinney Hill (2221 ft), to Bell Craig (2047 ft), a distance of some 2½ miles. A descent is best made by going back a little to the dip between Bell Craig and Andrewwhinney Hill, and then going diagonally down to the right towards the National Trust car park and the road. It is then 1½ miles up the road to Birkhill. Distance, about 6 miles.

8   Bodesbeck Law, White Shank, Capel Fell   PNRC*

Leave a car at Capplegill as in No. 2, and go down the track to Bodesbeck Farm. From it a path goes east, up the north side of the burn. Follow this path up to the watershed and turn left, following the county boundary for ½ mile to the top of Bodesbeck Law (2173 ft). Return to the watershed and follow the boundary south for ¼ mile, then west over an unnamed top (1858 ft) and then south to White Shank (2035 ft).

Continue south over another unnamed top (about 2100 ft) and on south-west for another half mile to Capel Fell (2223 ft). From there go down the broad ridge that runs a little north of west towards Sailfoot and cross the bridge there to the road about 1½ miles from the start. Distance about 8 miles. For a shorter round, Bodesbeck Law may be omitted, reducing the distance by about 1½ miles. Bodesbeck Law may also be climbed on its own, giving a short walk of about 4 miles. From near the top on Capel Fell on the full round, an impressive view south-east into the gorge of the Selcoth Burn is obtainable.

9   Croft Head, Loch Fell, Ettrick Pen   PNPC*

A car may be taken across the Moffat Water at Shortwoodend and left near Sailfoot or Selcoth. An old path leads from Selcoth along the right, south-west, side of the Selcoth Burn over to the Ettrick Valley. This path may be followed for some 2 miles to the corner where the Selcoth Gorge turns sharply from south-east to north-east. There is a steep bare slope here down to the burn and care is needed, but the view up the gorge is surprisingly wild. The path continues on the south side of the gorge for another mile up to the watershed at the county boundary. Alternatively, and with even better views of the gorge, when leaving Selcoth go up the slopes on the right to the summit of Croft Head (2085 ft). From this top a steep, curving, narrow ridge goes down towards the gorge and joins the path where it turns north-east, at a small, but conspicuous,round sheep fank. From this sheep fank at (160 059) go south-east up a steep grassy slope, over a small bump and on for another ½ mile to the top of Loch Fell (2256 ft). From here follow the ridge north-east for 1½ mlies, down and up to Wind Fell (2180 ft). Continue east and then north to Hopetoun Craig (2075 ft) and finally for another mile down and up to Ettrick Pen (2270 ft), the highest hill on this side of the Moffat Water. The quickest return is probably to go back over Hopetoun Craig and then due west to meet the Ettrick path a little north-east of the county boundary, and follow the path down from there to Selcoth. Total distance for the round, including Croft Head, about 10 miles. Omitting Croft Head does not reduce the distance appreciably, but reduces the ascent by some 600 ft.

· Many variations are possible on this circuit; on the ascent the path may be followed to the county boundary and Loch Fell approached direct from there, with a return north-west to the sheep fank in the dip; or the whole circuit may be reversed, going to Ettrick Pen first. The Selcoth Gorge looks particularly fine in snow conditions, but even more care is then needed.

Nickies Knowe to Talla

10 A Glen Walk–Wamphray Glen, Cornal Glen to Craigbeck TNT (X)

From Moffat go up the Moffat Water road (A708) for 1½ miles and turn very sharply down to the right to a bridge over the river. A car may be left here. A track goes off left and then up the hillside to the right, then left again and winds up the picturesque glen of the Cornal Burn, climbing all the way to 1307 ft after about 3½ miles. Here it goes in a great semicircle downhill, passing two side glens on the north side and, after another ½ mile, reaching the ruins of Garragill, at the edge of the forestry plantations. The walker is now at the head of Wamphray Glen and for the first half mile south there is little sign of a definite path. The path is at first on the west side of the burn and soon becomes a track and then at Laverhay a road (140 981). A car can be brought to here to meet the walkers, or another 2 miles down the now wooded glen brings you to Wamphray, some 6 miles south of the starting point. This walk may, of course, be done in the opposite direction, and the views look surprisingly different. At the most northerly point of the route the walker is about 1½ miles south-west of the summit of Loch Fell, which could be climbed from there. Distances: Moffat Water Bridge to Laverhay, about 8 miles; to Wamphray, 10 miles; to highest point (1307 ft) and back, 7 miles.

11 Black Esk Reservoir TC

From Lockerbie go along the Ettrick road (B723 for some 10 miles, past Boreland to Sandyford (204 947), where a road goes off on the left at some houses. A car may be left here—it is a pleasant walk up the forest road—or taken another 2½ miles to the dam at the foot of the reservoir. An attractive walk is to go round the reservoir on forest tracks. Cross the dam to the east side and after a short path get on to the track that runs up the east side. Turn sharp left at a junction after the end of the reservoir is passed in about a mile, and follow the track for another mile to where it goes left. Here cross the burn at the edge of the forest, to the road on the other side to Garwaldshiels. Turn left and go down the track on the west side of the reservoir back to the dam. Distance: from Sandyford round the reservoir and back, about 7-8 miles; from dam round, 3-4 miles.

12   Grey Mare's Tail to Tweedsmuir   PNR(X)*

This is a very fine through route. From the Moffat Selkirk road, A708, follow the path into corrie of Loch Skeen, and cut across to the left on to White Coomb. Keeping to the highest ground, go west to Firthhope Rig and turn north over Donald's Cleuch Head and Firthybrig Head. From here turn north-west still keeping to the highest ground, on to Molls Cleuch Dod and continue to Carlavin Hill overlooking Talla reservoir. The descent here is best made a litte east of north to avoid the steepest slopes to the road. The road is then followed past the reservoir to Tweedsmuir. Distance, 10-11 miles.

13   Megget, Lochcraig Head, Great Hill, Talla   NTRC*

This is a fine, rewarding, but long round. It starts from the Megget Stone at the summit of the road from St. Mary's Loch to Tweedsmuir. Follow the rather twisting boundary dyke south, then east and south-east to Nickies Knowe (2493 ft) and continue south-east then south to Lochcraig Head (2625 ft). This gives a fine view south-east down steeply to Loch Skeen. From here dip steeply down south-west and up again to Firthybrig Head (2504 ft) and then curve to the right to the broad round top of Great Hill (2541 ft). This looks down to Gameshope Loch, but it is better to descend north-west to the track in the Gameshope Glen and follow this track to Talla Linfoot. From here a steep mile on the road brings you back to the start. Distance about 9-10 miles.

14   Fruid, Garelet Dod, Din Law, Cape Law   RNC*

This is another long but attractive hill circuit. From the Moffat— Edinburgh road, A701; turn off at Tweedsmuir and almost at once turn again sharp right for Fruid. Cars are supposed to stop at the dam to the west end of the reservoir, but the road continues for some 2 miles to the group of houses at Nether Fruid. From here it is best to go straight on to the hill in a south-easterly direction, over Strawberry Hill and up on to Garelet Dod (2264 ft). From here half a mile south leads over the little bump of 2006 ft and on south for another mile to Din Law (2183 ft). The little Gameshope Loch is seen in the hollow below and may be visited. From Din Law the broad south-east slope is followed for about a mile to Cape Law (2365 ft). The return may be made by descending west to the glen of the Fruid Water and following it back to the houses at Nether Fruid. Distance (from the dam), about 12 miles.

SECTION 11
Dumfries, Lockerbie, Annan to the coast
1   Torthorwald, Tinwald Shaws, Torthwald   RTRC

Take a car or bus to Torthorwald on the A709 road and turn into the long straight road on the left just before the top of the hill. After 2 miles, at Tinwald Shaws, a track goes up to the right, behind the farm, and in half a mile joins a similar track from Tinwald. Turn right and follow this pleasant woody track for ½ mile down and up to a crossroads at (029 813). Here turn right and follow this road downhill into Torthorwald. At the village you will see the line of the old Lockerbie road coming down from the left, before you reach the present road. Distance, 5 miles.

2   Tinwald, Damhead, Ferneycleuch, Tinwald   RTRC

Go by car or bus to Tinwald, just off the Moffat road A701. Just east of the burn a narrow road goes up steeply to the left (signposted) to Cotland and Damhead. This road curves pleasantly up past the two farms, giving fine views back to the south. From Damhead a track continues for a mile, going down very steeply at the end. Turn sharp right at the foot of the hill, past Bruntshields and continue for half a mile to the road near Ferneycleuch. Turn right here and go about a mile south to the crossroads in No. 1 above. Here turn right again and follow the track west for 1½ miles back to Tinwald. Distance, 5½ miles.

3   East Tinwald, Tinwald, Locharbriggs   RTR(X)

The start of this walk is about 6 miles out from Dumfries on the Lockerbie road A709. A narrow road goes off on the left here at (048 809). After half a mile go straight on at a crossroads; do not turn right to Skipmyre. In another ½ mile the crossroads of Nos. 1 and 2 is reached. Again go straight on for another 1½ miles to Tinwald. Turn left at Tinwald and reach the Moffat road A701 at the outskirts of Locharbriggs. Bus services are available to both ends of this walk. Distance, 3 miles.

4   Glencaple, Bankend, Kirkconnell Lea, Glencaple   RC

Go by car or bus to Glencaple by the B725 road that runs along the east side of the Nith from Dumfries. From the corner at Glencaple a road goes straight uphill past the school as in Section 1, No. 11. Follow this for the 1½ miles to the War Memorial and turn right for about ¼ mile, then right again (before reaching Bankend village). This road leads over, in about 2 miles to Kirkconnell Lea, on the shore road and gives good views over the Nith estuary, the Solway and the Criffell hills. At Kirkconnell turn right again along the shore road back to Glencaple. Distance, 6 miles.

5   Across the Lochar Moss   TP(X)

Go by car or bus to Collin on the A75, Annan road, and then along the 'Low Road' (B724) towards Mouswald. At a crossroads about a mile before Mouswald, at (053 734) a track goes down to the right towards the railway, and in ¼ mile passes under it. This track continues south-west, keeping on the east side of the Wath Burn, deteriorating into a path and coming, in some 2 miles, to Horseholm Farm. The track from the farm forks and continues for another mile to reach the Bankend road, either ½ mile north or ¼ mile east of the village. Distance, so far, about 4 miles. A return can be made to Dumfries by car or bus from Bankend, but if the walk over the remote quietness of the Moss has been found to be pleasant, a return to the start may be made from Horseholm, giving a walk of about 6 miles.

6   Brow Well, Ruthwell, Bowerhouses, Clarencefield   RTRC

As in No. 5, go along the 'Low Road' (B724) to a point about a mile before the old Ruthwell station, at (077 705) where a road goes off on the right past South Bowerhouses and on past Longbridge-muir. Go round the farm and continue by a track south-east towards Comlongon Woods. Where the track reaches them turn right and continue for another ½ mile or so to the coast road near Cockpool. Here turn left and in about a mile, beside a small bridge, is the 'Brow Well'. This chalybeate spring was visited by Burns during his last illness. Another mile brings you to the village of Ruthwell, where the Duncan Museum of the first Savings Bank (founded there in 1810) may be visited. Taking the second turning on the left here, and crossing the Annan road, brings you in ½ mile to Ruthwell Church with its celebrated cross, which can be seen inside the church.

114

Turning left for about ¼ mile brings you back to the Annan road. A right turn there and a 2 mile walk past Clarencefield brings you back to the starting point. Distance, about 7 miles. If Ruthwell is omitted, about 1½ miles less.

7   Lochmaben, Hartwood, Torthorwald, Lochmaben   RTRC

From Lochmaben go along the B7020 road to the south, on the west side of the Castle Loch. The Castle Loch is one of the three local lochs which have the rare fish, the vendace; near the south end of the loch the road crosses the Vendace Burn coming in from the right. At the end of the loch a track on the left goes down, for ¼ mile, to the ruins of Lochmaben Castle on a promontory. Cotinuing on the B7020 road, for 2 miles from Lochmaben, turn right at a junction at (087 798). Go straight on, south-west, at crossroads, passing Muirfield Farm. The road now goes steeply uphill and passes Hartwood and on through trees to emerge on the high ground of Carthat Moor. The track continues south-west, over a crest and down to Linns on the road to Torhorwald. Turn right for a little over a mile to reach Torthorwald. A bus can now take the walker back to Lochmaben. Distance, Lochmaben to Torthorwald, 7 miles.

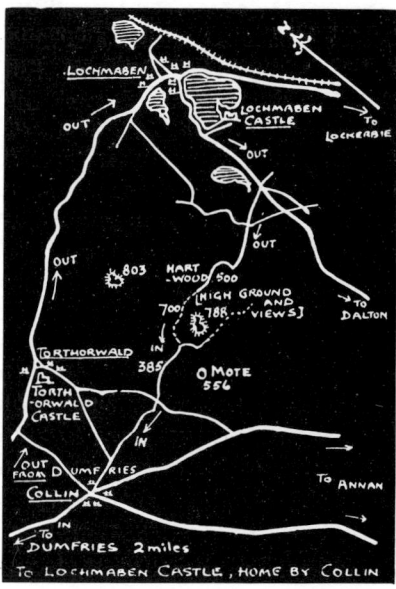

8 Breconrae, Holmains, Carthat, Breconrae RTNTRC

Go out the Annan road A75, by car or bus, to junctions at Breconrae (058 749). With some difficulty a car may be left somewhere near here. Walk up the road on the left of the main road, passing Mouswald Banks and continuing up and over a crest for nearly 2 miles. Turn left at a downhill junction and in another mile left again up the track to Kirkhill. On the left here the ruins of Little Dalton Church, a very old pre-Reformation church, are to be seen. Follow this track for another 1½ miles uphill to the derelict buildings of Holmains. Go past Holmans on the left and keep on the track for perhaps another ½ mile. Do not follow a path that veers off to the right here; go north-west for about a mile, aiming for the most westerly corner of the forest and keeping outside it—there is little sign of any path here, and the going is rough. At this corner is a very small secluded loch. Continue north-west, towards the edge of the forest, and you will come to the track of No. 7 from Hartwood to Linns. Turn left and follow this as in No. 7 to Linns (045 765). Here turn left and in 1½ miles return to the starting point at Breconrae. Distance, about 9 miles.

9 Hoddom Castle and Hoddom Bridge TPC

On the B725 from Dalton several Nature Trails and Woodland Walks, varying in length from half an hour to two hours in duration, are laid out in the woodland around Hoddom Bridge and Hoddom Castle Caravan Park. These walks start from a picnic area at Hoddom Bridge and include the woodlands of Woodcockair, Repentance Tower and Hoddom Castle. It is well worth the physical effort of climbing to the top of Woodcockair and to Repentance Tower from which can be seen good views of the Solway Coast, Cumbria and Annandale.

The walks afford the naturalist a chance to see a variety of birds, animals and flowers. For others the quiet and beauty of the scenery will be ample flowers. For others the quiet and beauty of the scenery will be ample reward. Some of the walks, especially the climb to the top of Woodcockair, are not recommended for the very young or the less spritely. However, with the variety of walks there is something to suit all requirements.

10   Birrenswark or Burnswark Roman Camp   TPNTRC

This striking flat-topped hill is a conspicuous landmark for many miles around, and consequently it commands a very wide view. The Roman camp is thought to be a successor to earlier fortifications on the site. The hill is some 4 miles south-east of Lockerbie and is 920 ft above sea-level. The nearest approach by car is probably by the side road going north from Ecclefechan some 2 miles almost to the foot of the mound. But a more attractive approach on foot is from the north. Leave Lockerbie by the Langholm road (B7068), and after about 3 miles, at Tundergarth, a car may be parked. A track goes off here to the right, south-east, towards Hazelberry, but in ¾ mile, before reaching Hazelberry turn south on a path to Oxwhite, past a small wood and straight on to Burnswark Hill. From the top a return may be made by the same route, but a good circuit may be made instead by going down the east side of the hill, past Stockbridge and turning left. Two miles along this road to the north brings you to the Langholm road again, about 1½ miles from the start at Tundergarth. Distance, round 6-7 miles. Distance, Tundergarth and back, about 4 miles.

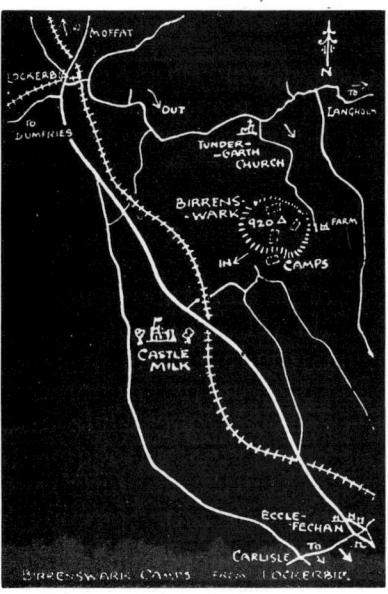

11   Hazelshaw Hill and Blountfield   TNPTRC

From Dumfries a small radio mast is conspicuous on the skyline above Collin to the east. (There are actually two masts.) It is a pleasant walk to these masts, with good open views. Go about a mile past Collin on the Annan road (A75 and turn left; after about $\frac{1}{4}$ mile turn right, near West Mains, and in 250 yds a track will be seen on the left. A car may be left somewhere near here. This track winds up past Rockhallhead and a line is made up the hillside towards the masts. The stones of Rockhall Mote can be seen going south-east along the ridge and down to a small reservoir (not marked on the maps). Go along this to the reservoir and turn right down the side of the little burn to Blountfield. At Blountfield the farm track goes right then left through the trees down to Breconrae on the Annan road. Turn right and go along this for 200 yds then fork right and take the side road back to the start in about $\frac{1}{2}$ mile. Distance, about $3\frac{1}{2}$-4 miles. Starting the walk from Collin would increase the distance by about 3 miles. It should be noticed that from the radio masts a second small reservoir can be seen in the trees above Rockhall Hotel. A descent can easily be made in this direction if desired, giving a shorter round.

12   Raehills, Minnygap, Mollin, St. Ann's   RPRC

Go out the Moffat road A701 for some 12 miles to a lay-by shortly before reaching St. Ann's Bridge (or by the Moffat bus). A narrow road goes up sharply to the left just before the bridge and the lodge at the private entrance to Raehills estate. After a half a mile this narrow road branches. Follow the right branch, behind Raehills House. This section has very fine trees and roe deer are often seen. The road continues north for some $3\frac{1}{2}$ miles, up the glen of the Broadshaw Water and out on to the open moor near Minnygap Farm. Here it curves round and finishes by going south at the last house. Continue by a path south, over the Brunthass Burn and round the grassy hillside to a very clearly marked 'Earthwork' (047 952) just before crossing the Ogle Linn. Continue, always southward, for another mile, over another burn and down to Mollin. The grassy path is in places faint, but the line to follow is fairly clear. Turn left at Mollin and follow the tarred road for $1\frac{1}{2}$ miles back to St. Ann's. As well as being very varied in its scenery this walk is also unusually good for the variety of birds to be seen. Distance, 7-8 miles. Return route rough.

13   Barrs Hill Fort (016 833) RPN

This strikingly situated ancient fort is visible on the hillside when approaching Dumfries on the A701 road before Amisfield and it gives fine views north to the Moffat hills. The lines of the deep grassy motes are still clearly seen round its summit where there is also now a line of fine beech trees. It may be approached by leaving a car near Tinwald Church. Turn right over Kirkland Bridge and then left up the road to Catland and Damhead. After about a mile the metalled road ends at Damhead and a track continues uphill along a line of trees. The fort can be seen across a field on the left. After a quarter of a mile a gate on the left allows entry to the field and so up to the fort which is just past the line of beech trees. Distance from church about 2 miles each way.

SECTION 12
Wigtownshire

The A75 road to Stanraer may conveniently be taken to divide Wigtownshire into The Moors on the north and The Machars to the south. The highest point on The Moors is just over 1000 feet and the moors are open and undulating. Over this area there are many quiet side roads mostly quite good for cars, or for walking. But there is also attractive, though rough, walking to be had along much of the rocky coastline. Almost any side road to the west coast between Corsewall and the Mull of Galloway, or near Burrow Head, will lead to a picturesque but rough coast walk. A few of the many possible are mentioned below.

1 Stairhaven to Auchenmalg (209 537) NRC

From Stairhaven, two and a half miles south of Glenluce follow the coast, going above the broken ground on the shore if preferred, for about 2½ miles to Auchenmalg Bay. Return may be made to Stairhaven by the side road that branches left half a mile from the shore (233 522). About 6 miles.

2 St. Ninian's Cave (425 359) RTC

This is marked on Bartholomew's map (sheet 37) and on the 1 inch ordnance map. The Isle of Whithorn road (A747) should be left at the crossroads (438 381) and the narrow road to Physgill followed, with some twists, to the shore in about two miles. The route is signposted and although a car can be taken part of the way, it is a pleasant woody walk. Distance back to crossroads, about 4 miles.

3 Burrow Head TNTC

The three miles of coast south and west of Isle of Whithorn towards Burrow Head gives a pleasant and picturesque walk, some of it on turf slopes above the sea. It is possible to start by a path along the shore from Isle of Whithorn, or to go down to the shore a mile or so west by a side road to Morrach. There is now a caravan site on part of the slopes here. The rock scenery becomes wilder as one approaches Burrow Head. A return may be made by the inland track past Cutcloy to Isle of Whithorn. Distance, about 6 miles.

4   Crammag Head   RTNC

Leave a car at the corner (094 349) of the side road near Knockencule, some 3 miles west of Dummore, and walk down a track past Slock Mill and out to the light at Crammag Head. The cliff scenery is very wild. A circuit can be made north to Portencorkie Bay, and a return made from there to the car, involving a round of about 3 miles, with the coast section rough going.

5   Clanyard Bay   TNTC

A car may be taken to Low Clanyard (108 374) and a track followed down to the attractive Clanyard Bay. If the shore is followed northwards for about a mile, an ascent east can be made to a track half a mile inland leading back to Low Clanyard. Distance, about 3 miles.

6   Port Gill and Port Logan   NTC

Half a mile north of Port Logan a side road on the left leads north-west for about 2 miles to Port Gill. The road is latterly rough and narrow but passable. A track from a corner at (080 430) leads to the shore and the coast can be followed north round Port Gill Bay, Port Lochan Bay to Druinbreddan Bay. From here a winding track leads inland in half a mile to the narrow road back to the Port Gill corner. The road is about 3 miles on the map. The going on the shore is rough.

7   Black Head and Killantringan   TNTRC

About 2½ miles north of Portpatrick on the coast road A764 at (000 575) a road on the left leads down in 1½ miles to the lighthouse on the Black Head, a striking viewpoint. After visiting the lighthouse the return track may be left half a mile north and a descent made to the shore at Killantringan Bay. A walk of a mile north to Knock Bay brings you to a track beside the stream. This leads back to the A764 road to Knock. Round distance, 5-6 miles.

8   Loch Ochiltree   RPC

One of the moste attractive parts of The Moors is on the road B7027 from Newton Stewart to Barrhill where several lochs lie near it. A farm road goes off north at (322 709) to Loch Ochiltree in abut 3 miles. From here, after visiting the loch and its adjoining Loch of Fyntalloch, a path south-west to the farm of Knowe (311 726) brings you back to the road. Distance, about 6-7 miles.

9   Port Gill to Port Logan   by the edge of the heughs   RNC

A car may be left at (098 412) where the road to Port Gill turns off to the left. This road leads past Munhill to port Gill in about 1½ miles. Here, before descending to the shore, turn left along the grassy edge of the heughs. There is no proper path for much of the way, but the going is pleasant and the views are fine, but there may be some obstacles in the way of fences and dykes. On a fine day the views are worth it. The route leads down eventually to the track that goes past the Logan Fish Pond and so back to the road junction or Port Logan. Distance 3-4 miles.

10   New England Bay to Balgown   NRC

A very short attractive shore walk. About 3 miles north of Drummore turn off the A716 at the New England Bay Camp Site where a car may be left. A few yards walk takes you to the beach. Turn left and go along the beach to the north. At high tide the beach is stony, at low tide there is a fine expanse of sand. After about a mile a track goes from the cottages on the shore inland to the farm of Balgown and continues to the A716 again, some 1½ miles from the start Distance about 3 miles.

11   Carleton Shore   RTNC

This is a walk for those who wish to do some beachcombing on an isolated shore. Take the coast road A747—A750 between Isle of Whithorn and Port William to a cross road at (402392) near Craiglemine. Turn coastward by a rough farm track towards Carleton. A car may be taken for perhaps a mile, or the car may be left at the cross roads. Continue on foot past the houses at Carleton by a track that leads diagonally down to the beach on the right, north side. The beach is very rough, remote and has rocky pools, birds and enough flotsam to keep the most eager beachcomber busy. Return by the same route. Distance 3 to 4 miles.

12   Garlieston–Eggerness Point   TPNC

A car may be left at the north end of the bay at Garlieston where a private road to Eggerness goes off. A path leads off to the right along the shore, at first in the trees then on the open shore among the stones. It gives pleasant views across and out of the bay. Some parts of the path are very rough and in summer can be plagued with brambles and bracken. From the point the return is made by the same route. Distance 2 miles.

Those who are very energetic may continue round the shore for another rough $1\frac{1}{2}$ miles to the road end at the very attractive little beach at Innerwell Port, where it could be arranged for a car to pick them up.

APPENDIX

When you go to the hills, always take with you a 1 : 50,000 Ordnance Survey map. On lower ground a half-inch is enough, and covers a greater area on one sheet. And always take a serviceable pocket compass as well. When you see you are about to enter or be overtaken by the mist, look up your objective—note its direction on the map—say, N.E., or a little to the south of S.W.; then take out your compass and walk through the mist with confidence, constantly checking your direction by consulting the compass.

Note on Map References. These are given using the standard 6-figure grid reference. As an example, the position of point A is obtained by first reading the number on the vertical line on its left, 73, and estimating the number of tenths of a division from that line towards the right—say eight-tenths, giving 738. Then, similarly, read the number on the horizontal line below the point, 22, and estimate the number of tenths up to the point, say three-tenths, giving 223. The full 6-figure reference is then (738 223).

Another thing you must attend to is clothing. You must have a waterproof anorak or cagoule with a covering for the head, light if possible, but sure to keep out the rain. Also you should take in your ruc-sac, almost at any season if you are going high up, some spare woollens—a pullover, a scarf, a pair of gloves. Until experienced, one could hardly credit the extreme difference of temperature and of wind velocity which may be met with in mounting from a sheltered glen, to a summit over the 2000-foot line. You may get very hot, and perspire freely, and then you may sit down for a lunch on a cold rock on an exposed col, and find yourself a-shiver before you have half-finished. A few woollies are very light to carry, and if not needed (some summer days, of course, are warm at any height), well, there is no harm done. But suppose you *did* happen to lose your way and have to spend a night out!

Always take a little more food than you need, rather than a little less, and in winter take a hot drink, or soup, in a flask. You may be out hours longer than you expected—a 'snack' is a fine pick-me-up.

Many experienced hill-men never carry a walking stick; but the writer would not be without one on these excursions.

The climbs and routes are not concocted from maps. The writer has stood on all the summits mentioned, and gone to them by the routes given—many of them, too, in the winter months. They are therefore guaranteed quite practicable.

Note for those visiting the Burns Country

The various places of interest to Burns lovers in Dumfries district are to be found, each in the section appropriate.

Burns' Walk on the Nith, Section 1, No. 1.

Burns' farm of Ellisland, Section 1, No. 13.

Brow Well, where he spent almost his last days, Section 11, No. 6.

Burns' House (open daily), where he died on 21st July 1796, is in Burns Street, near St. Michael's Churchyard, where his tomb is sheltered by the famous Mausoleum.

Burns Centre (open daily) is opposite the Whitesands.

INDEX

127

128

129

FORESTS OF THE SOUTH WEST

The Forestry Commission began tree planting in Galloway in 1922 and now many thousands of acres of forest often amid splendid scenery are available for the visitor and the walker to enjoy.

Walkers are welcome to make use of any roads and paths within the forests some of which give access to open ground and splendid view points. The Galloway Forest Park covers 250 square miles and was opened in 1943 recognising the special need for public access and for conservation and over a third of the area has been left unplanted. The tree covered areas are working forests and care should be taken near harvesting to avoid disturbing livestock or damaging crops when crossing agricultural ground.

Waymarked walks and trails offer walks of varying lengths and hardness but something for all people of all ages. Further details are available in "Galloway Forest Park — A Short Guide" and separate trail leaflets available from Tourist Information Centres and Forestry Commission Offices in the area.

Walks are also available from Mabie and Dalbeattie and the Forest of Ae all near Dumfries. Fleet Forest outside Gatehouse of Fleet offers attractive easy walking while Glentrool and Kirroughtree are good centres for a number of walks amid attractive scenery.

The Southern Upland Way crosses the Galloway Forest Park between Bargrennan and Dalry and thence on to Moffat. For the caravanner and camper Caldons Campsite near Bargrennan, 13 miles north of Newton Stewart makes a good base for the Southern Upland Way and other walks in the area. The simple but very attractive campsite at Talnotry adjacent to the Queensway, the A712 between Newton Stewart and New Galloway is another good centre for walking and an opportunity to see red deer and feral goats on the Deer range and Wild Goat Park near the Galloway Deer Museum at Clatteringshaws.

Further details on Walking, Fishing, Caravanning, Camping, Holiday Houses and other facilities are available from the Forestry Commission, 55 Moffat Road, Dumfries 0387 69171.

 Forestry Commission

NOTES

———

NOTES

NOTES